Castles in the Sky

Anita Cukier

BookLocker

Saint Petersburg, Florida

Published by BookLocker.com, Inc., St. Petersburg, Florida.

Printed on acid-free paper.

BookLocker.com, Inc.
2021

Cover Design: Aron Cukier
Editing: Shane Cullen

I would like to thank my husband, Aron, my editor, Shane Cullen, Monique Halpern, and my best friend Ala Konar for their constant and unwavering support. I could not have written this book without you.

I dedicate this book to our children, Ben, Eve and Mark, and our Grandchildren, Wolf, Mia, Ephram, Noa, Aiden, Kira, Emma, Sammie and Levi. I hope it will give you a glimpse into the past, something I never had but craved while growing up.

In memory of my parents
Zosia and Bolek (Wolf) Bild

Contents

A Call to Fela

A few days after my mother's death, I called Fela, one of her closest friends from Poland, who had lived in Israel for many years. After conveying her condolences, a short silence followed, then she said "Your Mother shared a secret with me and made me promise I would share with you, but only after she died."

Before I could even take a breath, she added "I am too distraught right now, but I will call you in a few days"

I did not hear from her for more than a week and, as anxiety began to twist my stomach, I called. As soon as she picked up the phone, Fela told me that she and her husband had decided that I did not need to know. For two years, I called regularly and begged, only to hear the same. Then, suddenly, the phone was disconnected. A couple of my friends who live in Israel went to Fela's apartment to inquire, but no one had seen Fela or her husband for a while and did not know what had happened to them. I tried to convince myself to forget about the secret since it was very unlikely that I would ever find out what it was. But I could not and still cannot. What could have been so terrible that my mother could not share it with me while she was alive?

Both my parents were Holocaust survivors. Unknowingly, they were in Auschwitz at the same time and both escaped before its liberation. They met right after the war and married very soon after. I was born ten months later. They were as different as night and day. They should never have married.

I found out that my father was in Auschwitz when I was about five years old. One day, I saw him crying as he was rubbing the number 126791 tattooed on his arm. When I asked "What is that on your arm?" he hugged me, and gently explained "During the war, I was in a place called Auschwitz. It was a very bad place run by bad people who tattooed all their prisoners"

"What is a prisoner? Did it hurt?" I asked.

"When you are older, I will tell you more about it, but right now let's have some cake."

When I asked my mom if she had also been in a camp, she enthusiastically suggested we read the new book she just bought for me.

But I knew that she was, because any time I complained about my food, she would say "When I was in Auschwitz I would have given everything for even one bite of what you are eating!"

I was a curious child, and, over the years, I made many attempts to get more information from my parents, but to no avail. I finally stopped probing because at some point I realized that it was painful for them to talk about it. After a while, I just forgot about it. When we moved to Australia I slowly learned much more, but it was not until I was in my early twenties, after I moved to the US, met other children of survivors and read many books about the Holocaust, that I began to fully comprehend how that horrific experience had affected my parents' lives. And how appropriately the term 'survivor' described those who lived through the Holocaust.

Now, faced with my mother's secret, *the* secret, I keep asking myself if it had something to do with Auschwitz? When they refused to talk about the Holocaust, were my parents protecting me from the horrors of their experience, or, were they also guarding something else, something somehow even darker.

Throughout his life, whenever I broached the subject of the Holocaust with my father, he would simply hug me and repeat how lucky and very grateful he was that he survived. But I knew that he continued to have horrible nightmares and that his outward happiness and gratitude must have been juxtaposed with horrible memories. My Mother, too, refused to talk about it. She would cut me short, and say "It is something that I never think about anymore." I believed her. After all, she was a sorceress and had easily convinced not just me, but so many people, that if you want something hard enough, and believe you can make it happen, it will.

But now I wanted to know about the secret but didn't know where to start to look for the answers. My first instinct told me that it had something to do with my mother and that it was connected to the Holocaust, either the Łódź ghetto, Auschwitz, or both, and if I wanted to discover what it was, I should start my search there. I decided to write down everything my mother told me about her experiences during the Holocaust and everything I could remember about her from my own past, hoping that some clue lay hidden in my memories.

When I started writing, I soon realized how little I actually knew about my mother's past. There were so many questions I couldn't answer. Those questions began to plague my mind to the point that I began to feel as if my entire existence was crumbling around me. I needed to know the secret, even though my brother, my husband and all three of our children kept telling me that I was overreacting, and, whatever the secret might be, it did not change who I was. I wanted to believe they were right, but I had to know.

I shared my worries with my best friend, Ala, who was a Holocaust hidden child. She, too, agreed with my family "Forget it, how is it going to help you? It's your Mother's secret, something she obviously could not share with you while she was alive, so leave it alone now."

That's when the recurring dream began haunting me. A beautiful young woman appears in my bedroom, wearing an alluring red dress, her makeup very overdone. She motions for me to follow her. I find myself in a nightclub filled with men. She points to a chair; I sit down, and, as I make myself comfortable, she takes to the stage. Motioning to the piano player to begin, she takes the microphone in her hand and starts to sing. Her voice is beautiful and the melody is filled with such sadness or, perhaps, longing. I listen intently, but the song is in a language I do not recognize, except for the ending, a phrase in English, repeated over and over again "Secrets, secrets, oh, so many secrets!"

For days on end, the melody, and especially the haunting refrain, *Secrets*, echoed in through my thoughts. It was increasingly hard to concentrate and I kept forgetting where I left my things. One day, while imagining possible scenarios and answers to the secret, I forgot to turn the gas off when I was making dinner and burned it all.

I became convinced that my mother's secret would always haunt me. I had to know what it was and why she withheld it from me. What if there had been clues in front of me all the time, but I just missed them? Or worse still, I was afraid to face them? Is that the real reason I stopped asking questions while Mom was alive, when I still had a chance? Why did it take me years after she passed to really start searching for what the secret held? Because I suspected that it might be about me? What if I wasn't her child? Or my father's?

I kept reminding myself that whatever I discovered, no matter how shocking, would not change the fact that I have had and still enjoy a good life, and have wonderful children and grandchildren; no revelation from the past could ever change that. As I got deeper into my search, I began to doubt myself. I knew that whatever my parents shared with me might have been obscured by time and trauma and that time has also clouded my own memories. If I could not even be sure of my own memories, how would I even know if anything I discovered was true? I was poring over all the notes I had made since I heard about the secret, when I came across a quote from Elie Wiesel that made me realize that the pursuit of the secret was not the only, and perhaps not the most important, reason to record what I remembered of my parents and my own life:

"I believe firmly and profoundly that whoever listens to a witness becomes a witness, so those who hear us, those who read us must continue to bear witness for us. Until now, they're doing it with us. At a certain point in time, they will do it for all of us."

Though the secret still occupied my thoughts and guided my search, I told myself that even if I never solved the puzzle of the secret, I would at least give our grandchildren a glimpse into my parents and my own past. When the older ones studied Holocaust at school, they had asked many questions about their great grandparents that I could not answer. I wanted my grandchildren to know more than I did about the family; something I had yearned for throughout my childhood.

Oranges and a Memorable Dinner Party

My mother was a seductress, a Pollyanna, and a magical storyteller. Her imagination was the world she lived in; our kitchen and living room were her stage.

When I was about seven years old, she took me to see Zbigniew Kurtycz, one of Poland's most famous singers at the time. We were late getting there and were pushing through to get to our seats just as he was walking onto the stage. Mom straightened up, turned to face him, smiled, touched her fingers to her heart and sat down, pulling me to my seat as well. Zbigniew Kurtycz bowed and then looking straight at her, dedicated his first song to the "Marilyn Monroe in the second row." The next evening, like many of the other performers whom Mom met, he was at our dinner table with ten or so other guests that Mom invited.

Every time Mr. Kurtycz came to visit, he would sit at the piano and sing his composition and my favorite *"Jade do Ciebie tramwajem"* (I come to you by tram) just for me. In my diary, he wrote "I hope that whenever you hear this song (I travel by a tram car to see you) you will remember how much I always liked playing and singing this especially for you."

In the kitchen, Mom easily convinced me and all my friends that she transformed into a wizard with a magic wand instead of fingers. We never doubted it, for everything she prepared tasted like enchanted potions, especially the apple slices covered in crisp dough and drizzled with honey, cream puffs as light as a feather and made with some "secret" ingredient, and, my all-time favorite, apple cake with layers of soft chunks of caramelized apples, alternated with raisins and walnuts and then topped with a cinnamon streusel made with flour, butter, cinnamon and sugar.

Seated on the floor at her feet, with the lights always dimmed, we would eat such treats while my mother, assuming a theatrical pose, her voice filled with excitement, described heroes who always went to extreme lengths to help those in need. The heroes' names always changed—Soter, Apollo, Zeus, sometimes even Aphrodite—and the needs of the people were vastly different, but the ending never varied. Inevitably, all those heroes and heroines would find their way to a castle in the sky; a magical place, hidden behind the clouds and accessible only by those who truly believed in its existence. The journey to it was arduous and took time. It required courage, optimism, patience, determination and, most of all, imagination. But in the end, it was always found and the hero and those they saved lived happily ever after.

Despite being enchanted by my mother's fairytales, I remember little of them, aside from a feeling of awe and fascination. However, there is one story she told that I never forgot. It was unlike any story I heard when I was a little girl and it all started when a mysterious crate arrived at our door one day. The wooden crate, with HARTWIG printed in bold letters, was filled with fragrant, perfectly round orange globes, as well as some smaller and less regular ones, each carefully wrapped in delicate tissue stamped JAFFA. Neither my mother nor father had any idea who might have sent the oranges.

As Mom very gently separated the peel from the flesh, an intoxicating aroma filled the room and teased my taste buds. Salivating, I waited impatiently until she offered it to me and soon I was rewarded with a flavor that was sweet yet slightly tart. I cannot recall how old I was at that time, yet the taste of the exotic fruit stayed with me forever and has become my own madeleine. While my parents debated about who the sender could be, I could only think about how my best friend, Richard, would react when he tasted it.

Holding one orange and one mandarin in each hand, I waited for him outside our building. The street was the center of our universe. There, we drew with chalk, played ball, and skipped rope. But on that particular morning, the Saturday before Easter, none of my friends were out and I thought that maybe I was too early. When the street finally filled with people, I noticed they all were all carrying very colorful baskets. As soon as I spotted my friend Richard, I ran to greet him and handed him the oranges, then offered to hold his basket. It was filled with intricately painted eggs and I reached for it very carefully. But before I had a chance to take it, I heard his mom shriek "No filthy Jew will touch a basket that was just blessed by a priest." I looked around to see who that filthy person was, but everybody was very clean and dressed in their Sunday best. By the time I turned back, the oranges were on the ground and Richard was being dragged away.

Some older kids, pointing at me, started chanting, "You filthy Jew, go back to Palestine".

Terrified, I kept asking, "What is a Jew?" as I ran home, crying all the way. Daddy got very angry when he heard what had happened and began to explain, but Mom would not let him. When he got up to speak to Richard's mother, Mom stopped him. She waved her beautiful hand as if to shoo away my questions and, with her characteristic, enigmatic smile, told me that I should forget this whole incident. But I couldn't and relentlessly asked her for an explanation. I needed her to tell me what a Jew was.

"Jews are people who don't go to church," she said as she turned to walk away. I was confused.

"But we do go to church sometimes. To hear the music at midnight mass on Christmas Eve." I reminded her "And what is Palestine anyway?"

Her face lit up as she began describing the tropical paradise that was Palestine, or Israel, as it was called now. A country where Jews grew the best oranges in the world, on dusty, hot deserts that they miraculously turned into orange groves, with green trees laden with fragrant orange globes. I became so engrossed in the story that I easily forgot the unpleasant confrontation.

Several days later, when a letter arrived explaining that the mysterious crate filled with oranges was sent by someone called Bronka, Mom was elated. Her friend Bronka was alive and well, and she was getting married! As Mom danced with me around the kitchen, she told me that Bronka was a woman she met during the war. They lost touch, but now Bronka had found her with help from the Red Cross. She thought Mom would like to know that she was going to be married. For a while, my mother repeated that phrase over and over again, and then, for reasons I did not understand, she began crying. When she finally stopped, she gaily announced that we were going to throw a party to celebrate the happy event.

Flushed with excitement, she planned the menu and then put out all the ingredients she needed for that night's dinner. For the first time ever, I was permitted to stay in the kitchen while she prepared the meal. As I watched her move swiftly from the cutting board to the kitchen sink, then to the stove and back, I could not help noticing how different she was to other mothers. How easily all this came to her! How happy she was all the time! While she prepared a special dinner for twenty, I begged for a story, as she had often told me and my friends, but she said that instead, this time I should just watch her and learn.

Within minutes, her immaculately manicured hands turned the chopped veggies, beans and a few bones into the most delicious smelling soup. The leftover mashed potatoes from last night's dinner became fancy gnocchis, while the swirled mixture of flour, eggs and milk, poured onto a hot frying pan, produced perfect, delicate crepes. Some she filled with a little meat, leaving others for dessert, to be served with fruit soaked in cognac and topped with whipped cream. A goose was already in the oven and the side dish of red cabbage stewed with apples, prunes and raisins was to be prepared next.

As we set the table and carefully picked up the right serving dishes, she shared a special secret with me "Setting the table is a creative process and it is even more important than the food preparation. Remember, no matter how delicious food is, it can only make your taste buds happy when it is presented in an attractive, creative and innovative fashion, and every sense in your body is then awakened— because now your meal has been transformed into a piece of art."

I was allowed to take out her beautiful china, and the white, delicately embroidered tablecloths and napkins to match. Next, she showed me how to make a centerpiece.

"This time," she said, "we will use calla lilies with the stems cut off and small pine branches"

In the cabinet in our living room, she found a long, oval crystal bowl.

"We will now cover the bottom with orange and yellow huge glass beads and fill it with water and then you will put the flowers in."

While she was talking, she took out the silver cutlery and fluted crystal glasses for the champagne, which I was not allowed to handle.

"Now, you can place the tiny orange vases, filled with only one calla lily beside the flutes"

I did all this very carefully and was admiring the table, when Mom whispered in my ear "For a truly festive effect, I will now place candles around the room"

She placed them all in her treasured crystal and silver candle holders.

Once the meal was over, Mom was showered with even more compliments than usual after her dinner parties. But, instead of basking in the adoration, as she had many times before, she somberly announced that she would like to tell her guests a story that might help them understand the reason for that evening's celebration.

At this point, I expected to be told to go to my parents' bedroom and go to sleep, as I was told after every dinner party, but this evening it seemed that Mom forgot all about me, so, very quietly, without drawing anyone's attention, I curled up on the carpet, next to the sofa.

Dance of Death

She began by reciting a poem, Goethe's 'Dance of Death,' in German. Oblivious to everything around her, her sweet and melodic voice made each verse sound like a song. Her guests were mesmerized, though I am sure no one could understand a word.

Der Totentanz

Der Türmer, der schaut zu Mitten der Nacht
Hinab auf die Gräber in Lage;
Der Mond, der hat alles ins Helle gebracht;
Der Kirchhof, er liegt wie am Tage.
Da regt sich ein Grab und ein anderes dann:
Sie kommen hervor, ein Weib da, ein Mann,
In weißen und schleppenden Hemden.

Das reckt nun, es will sich ergetzen sogleich,
Die Knöchel zur Runde, zum Kranze,
So arm und so jung, und so alt und so reich;
Doch hindern die Schleppen am Tanze.
Und weil hier die Scham nun nicht weiter gebeut,
Sie schütteln sich alle, da liegen zerstreut
Die Hemdlein über den Hügeln.

Nun hebt sich der Schenkel, nun wackelt das Bein,
Gebärden da gibt es vertrackte;
Dann klippert's und klappert's mitunter hinein,
Als schlüg' man die Hölzlein zum Takte.
Das kommt nun dem Türmer so lächerlich vor;
Da raunt ihm der Schalk, der Versucher, ins Ohr:
Geh! hole dir einen der Laken.

Getan wie gedacht! und er flüchtet sich schnell
Nun hinter geheiligte Türen.
Der Mond, und noch immer er scheinet so hell
Zum Tanz, den sie schauderlich führen.
Doch endlich verlieret sich dieser und der,
Schleicht eins nach dem andern gekleidet einher,
Und, husch, ist es unter dem Rasen.

Dance of Death

The warder looks down at the mid hour of night,
On the tombs that lie scattered below:
The moon fills the place with her silvery light,
And the churchyard like day seems to glow.
When see! first one grave, then another opes wide,
And women and men stepping forth are descried,
In cerements snow-white and trailing.

In haste for the sport soon their ankles they twitch,
And whirl round in dances so gay;
The young and the old, and the poor, and the rich,
But the cerements stand in their way;
And as modesty cannot avail them aught here,
They shake themselves all, and the shrouds soon
appear
Scattered over the tombs in confusion.

Now waggles the leg, and now wriggles the thigh,
As the troop with strange gestures advance,
And a rattle and clatter anon rises high,
As of one beating time to the dance.
The sight to the warder seems wondrously queer,
When the villainous Tempter speaks thus in his ear:
"Seize one of the shrouds that lie yonder!"

Quick as thought it was done! and for safety he fled
Behind the church-door with all speed;
The moon still continues her clear light to shed
On the dance that they fearfully lead.
But the dancers at length disappear one by one,
And their shrouds, ere they vanish, they carefully
don,
And under the turf all is quiet.

Nur einer, der trippelt und stolpert zuletzt
Und tappet und grapst an den Grüften;
Doch hat kein Geselle so schwer ihn verletzt,
Er wittert das Tuch in den Lüften.
Er rüttelt die Turmtür, sie schlägt ihn zurück,
Geziert und gesegnet, dem Türmer zum Glück,
Sie blinkt von metallenen Kreuzen.

But one of them stumbles and shuffles there still,
And gropes at the graves in despair;
Yet 'tis by no comrade he's treated so ill
The shroud he soon scents in the air.
So he rattles the door-for the warder 'tis well
That 'tis blessed, and so able the foe to repel,
All covered with crosses in metal.

Das Hemd muß er haben, da rastet er nicht,
Da gilt auch kein langes Besinnen,
Den gotischen Zierat ergreift nun der Wicht
Und klettert von Zinne zu Zinnen.
Nun ist's um den armen, den Türmer getan!
Es ruckt sich von Schnörkel zu Schnörkel hinan,
Langbeinigen Spinnen vergleichbar.

The shroud he must have, and no rest will allow,
There remains for reflection no time;
On the ornaments Gothic the wight seizes now,
And from point on to point hastes to climb.
Alas for the warder! his doom is decreed!
Like a long-legged spider, with ne'er-changing speed,
Advances the dreaded pursuer.

Der Türmer erbleichet, der Türmer erbebt,
Gern gäb er ihn wieder, den Laken.
Da häkelt - jetzt hat er am längsten gelebt -
Den Zipfel ein eiserner Zacken.
Schon trübet der Mond sich verschwindenden Scheins,
Die Glocke, sie donnert ein mächtiges Eins,
Und unten zerschellt das Gerippe.

The warder he quakes, and the warder turns pale,
The shroud to restore fain had sought;
When the end,-now can nothing to save him avail,-
In a tooth formed of iron is caught.
With vanishing lustre the moon's race is run,
When the bell thunders loudly a powerful One,
And the skeleton fails, crushed to atoms.

In the hushed silence that followed, she told her story.

I was barely fifteen years old when the Germans invaded Poland and captured Kalisz almost immediately after. I was a happy and confident girl, doing well at school, and due to graduate from high school the following June, at barely sixteen. In the fall of 1940, I was to move in with my relatives in Berlin where I planned to enter medical school. I did not even think of applying to a university in Poland; in the early 1930s, the Polish government's policies blocked Jews from participating in higher education. Those who wanted to pursue it, and could afford to do so, were forced to move to Paris, Prague, or Berlin.

Luckily, we had many relatives in Berlin and I spoke fluent German, so the choice was obvious. I would live with some of my grandmother's family, the Neumans, who were very important people. All the expenses would be covered by my maternal grandparents, even the trips home for every vacation. But, my grandparents insisted that I volunteer at the local hospital during the summer before moving to Berlin, in preparation for medical school. My grandfather's best friend was the director there, and he not only agreed but promised to teach and mentor me. He did and thought I was a natural.

Unfortunately, my dream and idyllic existence vanished once our town was annexed by Nazi Germany soon after the invasion of Poland in September 1939. As rumors of deportations began and the Germans issued more and more anti-Jewish ordinances, my grandfather, at a great cost, acquired Aryan papers for the whole family, mine stating that I was twenty years old and a nurse by profession. His foresight paid off, for when Jewish children were forbidden from attending the local high school, I was able to secure a nursing position in a nearby town.

I loved everything connected to medicine and learned eagerly. The chief of the medical staff at that hospital, too, was a good friend of my family and taught me a lot. Soon I was able to inject medication, insert catheters, and treat wounds of various kinds, and, more importantly, I knew what to say when the Gestapo showed up. For almost a year, I managed to hide my identity, until I was denounced by a newly arrived Jewish patient who worked at the hospital where I had volunteered. That same day, my whole family was rounded up and we were all deported to the Łódź ghetto.

The living conditions in the ghetto were horrendous, inhumane. Trucks full of new victims arrived every day and those who could not work anymore were taken to a nearby concentration camp in those same trucks. Clean water was scarce, disposal of waste infrequent, and keeping clean impossible. Soon, diphtheria, measles and all sorts of skin diseases spread like wildfire.

The hospital was overflowing with patients needing care, so one day I walked in and asked the chief doctor if I could work there. He was only too happy to offer me a job. This was truly a godsend. I was issued a work permit and, at least in the beginning, I was occasionally allowed to leave the ghetto proper and could bring in food when none was available in the ghetto. Though the work was grueling and I worked fourteen hours a day, I was happy to be able to help my family and more importantly, to be with them.

That did not last long.

Eight months after entering the ghetto, while I was at work, heavily armed SS men on trucks pulled up in front of our building. After a thorough search of the building, aided by the Jewish police and their dogs, they rounded up my parents along with all the other inhabitants of that building, loaded them onto a truck, and drove them out of the ghetto. I learned about it much later from one of the guards, who also told me that all the transports that day went directly to Auschwitz.

Luckily, my ten-year-old sister was staying with a friend that night, and she did not share our parents' fate. I managed to hide her until the summer of 1944. She was killed during a surprise SS raid. The dogs found her hiding in our closet—when I came home her dead body was lying on the ground outside our building. According to one account, she was tossed out the window while she was still alive.

Only a few days later, together with the last of the hospital staff, I was deported to Auschwitz. As soon as we entered the camp, the female guard in charge shouted at us in German "Quick, get undressed and line up."

I took the opportunity and stepped out and quickly told her, "I speak German and I am a qualified nurse, so I can be of help."

The first kick to my back knocked me off my feet. More kicks followed rapidly.

"You little shit, you think you are better than the rest because you speak German? You are nothing more than a filthy, stinking Jew!" she kept screaming as she kicked me even more fiercely.

By then, I could hardly see through my tears and only heard the laughter as the other Germans joined in. Continuing to kick me, she grabbed my hair and dragged me, while repeating, "A filthy Jew who speaks such beautiful German, must indeed be singled out".

I must have lost consciousness since I had no idea where I was when I felt water pouring over my head.

"You will now clean the toilets," she screamed, and as an afterthought added "When you are done, you will clean my boots and if I want, you will lick them too. And you will do whatever I want and whenever I so desire!"

She threw some rags at me, brought a bucket with water, and locked me in. I tried to get up but I was in terrible pain and I threw up over the toilet floor. When I was finally able to get up and cleaned the floor and bent over to do the same with the toilet, the stench almost knocked me off my feet again, but I knew I had to get going. Gagging, I did the best I could. It seemed to take forever, but, finally, someone unlocked the door and barked to follow him.

He led me to a barracks that housed what seemed like a hundred women. Each bunk, if you could call a wooden plank covered with sour-smelling pallets of straw, alive with fleas and lice, a bunk, had to be shared by six women. As it turned out, I was one of the lucky ones, as I had only four bunkmates.

All the women were forced to share only one outhouse. No provisions were made for our personal hygiene. Once a week, we were lined up, outside, stark naked, while sneering German guards sprayed us with icy water from a huge hose and then covered us in a foul-smelling delousing powder. Most of the girls stopped menstruating a few months after they entered the camp. But those of us who still had their periods often walked around with blood running down our legs. The guards seemed to enjoy this—it gave them another excuse to scream at us, to hit and berate us. We had no soap, no sanitary napkins, not even rags. We were always hungry, worked to exhaustion, and worried constantly about how long it would be until we were all gassed.

The toilets I had to clean were used by the German doctors and nurses in the concentration camp's "hospital". The Germans used young and healthy prisoners for all kinds of medical experiments. Some of these were performed with no anesthetic, and on those already dying from starvation. During these procedures, they were sometimes forced to answer questions like what their weight was at the time they were arrested, and what medications they were taking at that time. As if all that wasn't bad enough, these perfectly healthy individuals were injected with phenol and then photographed to document each stage of their horrific deaths.

I could not help wondering how these medical professionals, educated at universities, immersed in the heritage of Goethe and Schiller, doctors who swore the Hippocratic oath, could have such a complete lack of respect for human life. Is it a wonder that with each day it became harder for me to remember that I was still human? No matter how hard I tried to hold on to the thought that at least I was alive, it was impossible to escape the fact that I could be sent to the gas chamber at any moment, at the slightest whim of any one of the guards. But I did not want to die. And so I refused to die!

When hunger corroded my stomach, I thought of happier times at home. I would just close my eyes and return to my house and my mother. In no time, I could smell and practically taste all the delicious dishes she prepared for her famous banquets. These memories were so clear and vivid they made me forget the bleak reality of my daily ration, two slices of bread and water.

When ripped carefully into quarters, each piece became a different delicacy and my nostrils were filled with the aromas of soup, spiced with saffron, a cheese soufflé, golden and delicate and so high that it took special skill to take out of the oven. A wild mushroom bisque, made from mushrooms so fresh that they were still covered with the morning's dew. And, best of all, the lamb. First soaked in a complex marinade, for a whole day, and then basted, it was slowly roasted in the outdoor pit, filling the whole neighborhood with aromas so pungent, everyone's mouth watered.

I would go through this routine day after day, choosing the menu in a deliberate, systematic way, the way my mother always did. I savored every bite and deliberately made my meal last a long time. Sated, I could then sleep. I soon invited others to share these exquisite meals.

During the day, I wordlessly recited the words of "The Dance of Death," "The Reunion" or "The Nearness of the Beloved" and repeated them at night to my bunkmates. Over and over, I recalled each word, with reverence, with love, blind to everything around me. At first, I roughly translated the poems, but soon I found there was no need for that at all. The words and the rhythm of the German text soothed my bunkmates and made them, too, forget the fear of impending death. I became so immersed in a world of beauty and poetry that I easily imagined I was traveling back in time, to my home, to my parents and the days when I was so innocently happy.

The five of us thus managed until the end of December 1944. By then, however, everything in the camp began to change. Prisoners began to disappear rapidly as more and more selections took place. The crematoria worked day and night, and, as the stench became unbearable, I could no longer delude myself. I waited for my turn to come.

I began reciting my beloved poems aloud even during the day since I no longer cared if anyone could hear me. That is how I met Dr. Schmidt. Hearing the "The Dance of Death," he stopped and asked if I could start from the beginning. With tears in his eyes, he told me that I had just brought a slice of a sane world back to him, a world that he had almost forgotten existed. He asked if I would recite to him again the next day.

For the next few days, he would bring me extra bread and sometimes even a piece of cheese and I would recite every poem I could remember. After that, we would talk. For the first time in months, I felt like a human being. During one of those conversations, I mentioned that I had been a nurse in my previous life and he asked if I would be willing to help him with a young Polish woman he was secretly nursing back to health.

The girl was skeletally thin and her huge brown eyes seemed completely devoid of life. She was very young, no more than thirteen years old, and, as I looked at her, I could only think of my sister. I approached her cautiously and asked in Polish "Jak się nazywasz? (What is your name?)"

No response.

"Mówisz po Polsku (do you speak Polish?)"

Still nothing.

I continued in Polish, "Ja mialam siostrę która byłaby w twoim wieku, ale ja zabili w getcie i ja bardzo za nią tęsknie (I had a sister who would have been your age by now, she was killed in the ghetto. I miss her so much)"

There was absolutely no acknowledgment that she heard me, and though I talked a lot, she did not respond.

Dr. Schmidt told me that she was one of the young girls used for the sterilization experiments. For months, her ovaries were exposed to X-rays, each one slightly different, just to see how long before she would become sterile. She got through these torturous experiments far longer than any other young woman there. But when she stopped talking or showing any reaction, the doctors lost interest in her and would have gassed her, if Dr. Schmidt had not been able to convince his superiors to have her transferred to him. While pretending that he was conducting experiments to find a cure for the burns and sores that developed as a result of the radiation, he had been slowly nursing her back to health for a month now.

For the next two weeks, I would meet Dr. Schmidt in her room, and together we tended to her wounds, while I recited Goethe's poems and Dr. Schmidt would sometimes join in. This was January 1945. More changes were taking place in the camp every day. Trucks filled with people were leaving every few hours, and long columns of prisoners were marched out behind them. Gunfire outside of camp was heard constantly and as it came closer, I saw guards deserting their posts and hopping on trucks leaving the camp.

And then, one day, I found the hospital too had been deserted, except for the very sick Germans who could not be moved. Dr. Schmidt, who would not abandon his patients, was still there as was the young Jewish woman who was miraculously getting stronger every day. Dr. Schmidt took me aside as soon as I walked into her room and told me that orders had been issued to exterminate as many of the prisoners as the crematoria could handle, and to kill the rest by any means possible. He thought it best for me not to go back to the barracks, but hide in one of the hospital rooms until he came for me. He had made arrangements to take me with him out of the camp the following day in a truck, along with two other Germans.

I knew I could never leave without my three bunkmates (one had died only two days previously), and could not leave behind the poor girl I looked after. I begged Dr. Schmidt to include them, too, in the plan. He could not, he explained, mainly because he did not think he could trust the other Germans that were leaving with him. I refused to leave without them and pulling the girl out of bed, I ran out to warn the others.

Throughout that day, the shouting, screaming and crying outside were interrupted only by gunshots that seemed to come from everywhere. By the end of the day, my three bunkmates were convinced we would die at any instant, and, terrified, they began reciting Kaddish. I suddenly realized that the mute girl had quietly joined in. When I asked, she finally told us she was from Krakow, her name was Bronka and that she was twelve years old. Before we could ask anything else, Dr. Schmidt appeared and led us all out.

We were too scared to ask any questions. He handed me a coat, a pair of man's pants, and boots, and as we got into a truck, he motioned for me to put them on. I don't know how many others were there, or how long we traveled. When the brakes squeaked violently and the car came to an abrupt stop, Dr. Schmidt signaled for us to leave the car. He whispered we could hide in an abandoned hut up ahead until the war was over, which he thought would be in a matter of days. He added a quick warning not to trust any Russians and was gone.

It was very dark and cold and we had trouble finding the hut. When we came across an empty barn, we decided to stay there. Exhausted, we fell asleep almost immediately, Bronka right next to me, holding my hand. When I woke up, the sun was high up in the sky. I cautiously opened the door, went outside, and was confronted by an eerie stillness. It was snowing ever so lightly. I shivered as I detected the familiar stench of burning flesh, and I realized that the flakes were not snow at all, but ashes carried by the wind from the crematoria. As the wind picked up, everything around me turned completely gray. I stood motionless and, for the first time in months, I felt an overwhelming sorrow.

I fell to the ground and, for the first time in four years, I allowed myself to cry.

I do not know how long I was there, but when I got up, the wind subsided slightly and the trees around me swayed back and forth in a solemn, rhythmic movement. Like mourners at a Jewish funeral reciting Kaddish, I thought. As I felt a strong gust and then another, I saw that dark clouds were moving in rapidly. It started snowing, gently at first, and then almost with a fury. The thick white flakes blurred my vision and soon everything took on a strange, otherworldly appearance. The world froze in time and nature joined me in the mourning ceremony, covering the human ashes in a white shroud, appropriate for a traditional Jewish burial. When the snow had stopped, and the sun's golden rays shone out through cracks in the clouds, the snow on the ground shimmered and flickered.

It looked as if thousands of candles were lit in memory of the innocent bodies so violently desecrated by cremation. I stood there motionless, fervently and desperately wishing I could believe in God, and asking him for a sign. When the earth suddenly began to tremble under my feet and I heard a terrible roar, I was convinced that He had heard me, and was going to reveal himself. That finally, He was going to put an end to this horrible world and that all those innocent souls, whose only crime was to be born Jewish, would finally be avenged.

Instead, it was the sound of hundreds of tanks coming to save us! I took off my coat and began waving it in the air.

I must have fainted, and when I opened my eyes, I was looking into a barrel of a gun. The soldier was shouting at me in Russian, a language I recognized, but did not know. He motioned for me to get up, shouting to his comrades, "Germanka" ("German, German"). Pointing at myself, I kept repeating in Polish "Ja jestem Polka" ("I am Polish"), but it seemed futile. He released the safety and I started to recite the Kaddish.

At the sound of those first Hebrew words, the soldier's eyes filled with tears, as he said "Yevreyka? A Yiddish maidel?" ("A Jew, a Jewish girl?")

He was now hugging me and as the other soldiers came out of their tanks, I grabbed his hand and, completely forgetting Dr. Schmidt's warning, I led him to the hut.

The four terrified girls were cowering in the corner. They looked from me to the Russian officer, not moving at all. The officer looked even more startled as he looked from me to the girls. Before I knew what was happening, he again pointed the gun at me, shaking his head and saying, "Oh, no, oh, no."

Looking at the sorry sight the girls presented, I suddenly realized what the Russian was thinking. I wore a fine coat and decent boots while the girls were barely covered by the filthy, striped uniforms, their feet wrapped in tattered rags. I was very thin, but the other four were walking skeletons. My blond hair was cut to the skin, but they were completely bald and their scalps were covered in sores and scabs. I had no idea how I would ever convince this man that I, too, was a victim and not the enemy.

Before I had time to think, Bronka threw herself at the officer and shouted something in Yiddish, beating him with her fists. The other girls joined in and the officer let me go. The girls were now talking all at once, in Yiddish. I had no idea what was said because I had never learned Yiddish. The soldier obviously did, for he and my friends talked for a long time, from time to time gesturing towards me. I heard the name Dr. Schmidt and Goethe mentioned several times and the officer kept giving me strange looks each time. I was immensely relieved when, in Hebrew, he asked my name and the names of my parents. When I answered without any hesitation, the tension was instantly diffused.

Every one of the soldiers wanted to do something for us and soon there was more food than we saw in years. Some offered us money and four of the officers, including the one who finally let go of my hand, took off their leather jackets and gently wrapped them around the shoulders of the shivering girls. Others took off their boots and offered the shirts off their backs. Despite their warnings to be cautious and not eat too much so soon after starving, we gorged ourselves on the canned meats they opened for us. Sure enough, our stomachs, unused to any real food, revolted almost immediately and we ended up retching it all up. Lyev, the first soldier I had met, suggested that we rest for a little before trying to eat again. He was anxious to help us in any way he could, but he and his soldiers had to get going.

The next morning, after a short discussion with his commanding officer, Lyev and another soldier drove us to an abandoned farmhouse nearby, where we washed and the girls changed into the clothes the soldiers donated. After we rested for a couple of hours, they drove us to Kalisz, my hometown. They dropped us off right in front of my house, which was miraculously intact and looked exactly as I had last seen it. After many hugs, kisses and promises that he would come back as soon as he could, Lyev and the soldier were off.

My four friends waited while I ran up the steps and knocked. The woman who came to the door was someone I had known all my life—she cleaned my parents' house and occasionally babysat for my sister. At first, I thought she did not recognize me, so I started to tell her who I was. Before I had a chance to finish, the door slammed in my face and I heard the woman yelling, "Get away, you filthy Kike, this is my house now. If you ever come back, I'll shoot you like a dog."

I pounded on the door again and again. I continued to scream and bang on the door and the racket I was making attracted the attention of the people in the neighboring apartments. Stone-faced and quiet, they looked at me without a hint of sympathy. I knew most of those silent faces, they had been my neighbors for many years, but their eyes betrayed no hint of recognition. Confused, I hurriedly walked away with my friends. I still did not understand.

When I tried my grandparents' house, there, too, a familiar face opened the door. Fearing a repetition of the previous scene, I quietly asked about my grandfather, but the man said he knew nothing. I apologized for the intrusion, and walked away. My uncle's house was no longer there and the lace store he owned was now a lumber yard. The people who worked there claimed they never heard of him. Bewildered, I sobbed uncontrollably and Bronka and the others wept with me.

Two young men stopped and asked if they could help in any way. Though they were both emaciated and only a hint of dark stubble covered their shaved scalps, they were both undeniably handsome and were dressed in clean clothes, far too big for them, but obviously well made. As I suspiciously looked from one to the other, the taller one asked if I was Zosia. He remembered me from the soccer matches between the Prosna and the Maccabee where he played defense. I had no idea who he was, but I did attend many such soccer games as my cousin Leon played for the Maccabee.

The young man, who was very handsome and seemed kind, introduced himself as Wolf. I lied that I did, indeed, remember him and briefly explained what had happened to us and then introduced my girlfriends. Without any hesitation, Wolf invited us to his house, suggesting we could stay there until we found our families. My friends accepted the invitation without waiting for my answer. His house seemed untouched by war. All five of us stood there, awed and unable to speak, especially when Wolf asked if we would like to take a bath and then brought out a big cake of soap and a huge load of pretty dresses and undergarments. In a quivering voice, he explained that these belonged to his sister and mother. He quickly changed the subject, explaining how to light the water boiler, and left.

I filled the bath with hot water and slowly submerged myself. Almost with reverence, I picked up a cake of soap and deeply inhaled its sweet scent. Lily of the valley? I took note of the clean, white towels folded by the side of the bath, the mirror in a gold frame, the combs, and various hairbrushes laid out on the vanity. Was all this opulence truly real? I felt dizzy and confused but was determined to enjoy it even if it was all just a figment of my imagination. So, I closed my eyes, willing the lovely scent to erase the ever-present stench of the crematoria in my lungs and kept repeating out loud "This is a cleansing bath, I will be relieved of my past!"

Once my friends were done with their bath and we all complimented each other on our appearance, we joined the boys in the dining room. A simple, but delicious dinner was laid out on the dining room table. Steaming hot potato soup, chicken and fresh, still-warm bread! It was a banquet the likes of which I had not enjoyed for five whole years. It is almost impossible to describe all I felt as I sat down to eat, bathed and really clean for the first time in years, dressed in clothes I had forgotten existed, and sitting at a proper dining table about to eat a real meal. I looked at my friends and I knew that they, too, could hardly believe our fortune.

Wolf told us about his homecoming experience. Wolf's father, anticipating what would follow, signed over the family house to an employee. When he returned to Kalisz, this woman welcomed Wolf like a long-lost son and offered to move out immediately after handing him the keys to the house. His neighbors, to whom the family entrusted all their valuables, including jewelry and furs, came as soon as they heard he was back, bringing everything intact, except for one fur coat, which, they tearfully explained, they sold to a farmer in exchange for some potatoes and flour to make bread for their starving children. They apologized profusely for selling something that was not theirs to sell and begged to be forgiven.

How was all this possible, given my own experience that day? Yet, I had to admit that the evidence was irrefutable. The lovely house, the food, the warm and caring older woman who took care to make us all feel comfortable. For the rest of the night, I drifted in and out of consciousness, never sure of what was real and what was not, except for Wolf. The six of us spent the next two days and nights talking. We talked with a candor that we would never again allow ourselves and the more we revealed about the humiliation we all suffered, the more connected we felt to each other. In the end, we all made a solemn pact to always be there for each other.

I had nowhere else to go and decided to stay at Wolf's until I could be reunited with my family. Bronka, too, wanted to stay. Her parents were gassed as soon as they entered the camp, as were her sister, brother and grandparents and she had no other family, and, besides, she did not want to leave me. My three bunkmates opted to go and look for their families as soon as they found transport to take them home, but, until then, they too would stay at Wolf's place. The next day I put up signs all over town with my new address. I visited the town hall three times a day even though the Red Cross only posted a list of survivors a couple of times a week and the list was always very scant. But I never lost hope and got angry when Wolf, who was always there with me, tried, very gently, to prepare me for the worst.

On June 1, 1945, when Wolf asked me to marry him, I accepted. My friends began planning the celebration almost immediately. Bronka insisted on helping my friends to make the wedding dress, and the finished product, made out of the lace curtains from the window in Wolf's bedroom, was done entirely by hand. It was beautiful. By some miracle, Lyev, the Russian soldier who had found us after our escape, arrived in our town the next day and I asked him to give me away. Ten days later, Lyev supplied enough food to feed the whole town, and enough vodka to make everyone drunk. And, to our surprise, he somehow managed to find a rabbi. No one knew where he found him, but it did not matter.

The celebrations, which took place on June 10th, 1945, and lasted for three days, marked the first Jewish wedding after the war in that town, and maybe even in the whole of Poland. Bronka stayed with us for a few months but then left for Palestine with a group of young Zionists who came to our town. I had not heard from her until today.

After the Dinner Party

I am sure my recollection of my mother's story is a combination of what I heard that night in Poland and a version I heard, many years later, when Bronka came to visit us in Australia. My Mother threw another dinner party, this one even more lavish than the one in Poland and, afterward, she told her guests the story of her and Bronka's meeting once again. I thought that version seemed shorter, but it was far more dramatic because Bronka was there, and when Mom finished, both were visibly shaken and on the verge of tears. But, when Bronka and I got up to comfort Mom, she quickly regained control and, as if nothing happened, smiled at us and invited us all to have dessert. When her guests tried to ask questions, Mom waved them away with her beautiful hand "Forget it, this past will now stay in the past."

After everyone left and I tried to talk to her, she turned her back to me, shook her head as if she could not believe I would do that, and just walked away. I thought that maybe Bronka would be willing to fill in some more details. She could not add anything at all, she told me. She was a child at the time and could remember only that a kind German doctor saved her from Dr. Mengele (*also known as the Angel of Death—notorious for the most inhumane experiments on twins*) and that she ran away with my mother. Before my mother had retold the tale of their meeting, Bronka had not even remembered the doctor's name!

The next day, I begged my mother to fill in the gaps that were troubling me, suggesting she must have left out many of the details because I distinctly remember being terribly traumatized after I heard her talk about it in Poland. I remember having anxiety attacks when I had to see my pediatrician, or saw anyone in a uniform and refusing to speak German, a language taught to me by my mother and my nanny. But, Mom, with fury I had never witnessed before, screamed "Stop it, it is all behind us. Why, of all people, would you want to rehash it?"

I think that the Australian version must have been a later iteration and, horrific as it was, had many gruesome details missing from the narrative. That is the only way I could rationalize the trauma and attacks I suffered after hearing the story in Poland. I must have either forgotten it or it has become a buried memory.

A few days later, I again tried to explain why I kept asking. She made no effort to reassure me. Instead, she angrily replied, "You are letting your imagination run wild. Those anxiety attacks had nothing to do with what you heard that evening! How could that be? You were far too young to understand any of it! Please stop this nonsense, neither I nor Bronka want to talk about it ever again."

Even though I wanted to ask if a child really has to understand things to be affected by them, I stopped myself. I now wonder if my mother refused to speak of it again because it was too close to the secret? Because she knew there were hints within that tale, imperceptible to a child, but not to an adult? How many other details did my mother withhold and maybe lie about? How many questions did she shoo away with that magical wave of her hand, which could have led to clues about the secret? Or, and it is just as likely, had her own memory of those events simply changed. It was a long way, and a long time, between her experiences in Auschwitz and her life in Australia.

These days, I am getting increasingly frustrated by the thought that I, too, have forgotten elements of important events from childhood. How many forgotten things and half-remembered incidents, things that have shaped me, have been lost? More worryingly, how many things do I think that I remember, that may not be exactly true? What are the chances that some forgotten or misremembered thing might have held the key to the secret?

Learning How to Imagine

One morning, long before the memorable dinner party, when I was very young, my parents woke me up very early and told me that we had to go and say goodbye to my German nanny, Rutie. She and her family were leaving Poland! Before we even reached the lane that led to her building, I saw a long, single line of somber people, marching away from their homes, stooped under the weight of the white bundles slung across their shoulders. Even at that age, I knew they were leaving, and would not be back. My beloved nanny, my Rutie, was with them.

I called her name and, when she didn't respond, I screamed. At the sound of my shriek, she turned, and, seeing me cry, she started crying too. She cried and blew me kisses, but did not stop moving. I wanted to run to her, to hug her, but I was told I was not allowed, that we would all be punished if I disobeyed. I could not understand why, and, today, though the memory is vague, I can still feel that confusion. I kept crying and trying to pull away, and only stopped after my parents promised me a trip to a cake shop where I could have two of my favorite rose jam-filled doughnuts. I can't remember much else, but I know I missed Rutie a lot because, for a while after, I would crawl into my parents' bed in the middle of the night and wake up immediately if they tried to move me. According to my parents, I would never remember anything about it the next morning. No one ever explained why Rutie had to leave and, certainly, not what happened that day.

Now I again keep asking if it is simply time that made me forget, or is something more sinister to blame? Did I suppress this and maybe some other memories because they were too traumatic? I did not know anything about ethnic cleansing until after I left Poland. Wałbrzych, the town my parents eventually moved to and lived in until we moved to Australia, was Waldenburg before the second world war and, at that point, had been a German city for almost 200 years. At the end of WWII, the town and surrounding area became part of Poland and the name Wałbrzych was restored. Ethnic cleansing soon followed, and the area was practically emptied of Germans. What I had witnessed, a few years later, was the last German exodus from the "recovered territories" (these were lands reappropriated to Poland—as compensation for territorial losses in the east that had been absorbed by the Soviet Union).

After the first forced resettlement of the Germans, their apartments were quickly filled by Poles who now wanted to come back from the east and anyone else who had enough money to bribe the authorities. My parents fell into the second category and thus were able to acquire one of those fully furnished apartments. My mother liked that no one knew her there, so they could begin a new phase in their lives. The fact that they were able to quickly find an apartment that was completely furnished was also a good reason. Much of Poland had been ravished by the war, with ruins everywhere, but Lower Silesia, being part of the recovered territories, was practically untouched. Now, considering the secret, I have to wonder what other reasons my mother and father might have had for moving somewhere where no one knew them.

The building we lived in was typical of that area. A stark, three-story, grey stone structure, it was covered in dark soot from the coal mines just outside town. I always thought that the small narrow windows facing the backyard made a face that resembled the strange neighbor who lived on the third floor and seemed to be forever suspiciously observing the world below. A massive wooden door, always wide open, led to a dark, cavernous entrance hall that forever smelled of urine, undoubtedly deposited by the drunks who frequented the bar across the street. Luckily, our apartment faced the street and had two large windows in every room. It was comparatively light and airy, unlike the apartments in the back that overlooked a garbage dump, an ever-present feature in most backyards, just like the rats that inhabited them. Rats were omnipresent in most parts of Lower Silesia. They weren't just in garbage dumps, but also in the deep cellars where coal was stored, in locked compartments, individually assigned to each tenant.

There was a small hallway that led to a large square living room on one side and a spacious bedroom on the other. The kitchen was large enough to accommodate a cupboard, a pine table flanked by four chairs, and a coal-fed stove, which occupied an entire wall. There was no bathroom in the apartment, so when we wanted to bathe, my father would pull a huge tin tub out of the hallway closet and fill it with hot water, boiled on the kitchen stove. A communal toilet, on every other floor of the three-story apartment building, was shared by the six families.

Toilet paper was mostly unheard of, so newspapers were always saved and treasured by all. For night emergencies there was a potty, which we used in the winter, when all the pipes froze and we could not flush the toilet. Yet, despite the rats and toilet situation, I never thought that I lived in awful conditions, or, in fact, that I lacked anything at all. I would venture to say that in the early 1950s, most of the ordinary Polish people did not even begin to realize that in other parts of the world most people had better accommodation and lived more comfortably. I certainly thought our apartment was much nicer than any other.

I slept on a fold-out divan in the living room, which was dominated by another coal-fed stove; this one made of white, intricately carved ceramic. An antique Bechstein piano took up one corner, while the other was occupied by a carved cabinet with glass doors, filled with sparkling crystal wine glasses and baskets made from hand-blown crystal. The walls were adorned with old paintings: a landscape, two portraits of somber men dressed in embroidered merchant attire, and a still life, all in gold frames. A deep red Persian rug, speckled with burnt orange and royal blue designs, and a dining table with eight chairs, completed the decor of the room.

Each wall in that room, one coppery yellow, one light chestnut brown, one burnt orange, and one cherry red, took on a different hue at different times of the day and at night, especially on cold evenings when Daddy lit a fire in the coal stove. As we snuggled in bed, Mom would show me how the glowing embers transformed the room. Turning off the lights, she would point to the now dying fire "Look at the color of the embers and then look around the room. Do you see how different it looks in this light?"

I did not, but knew better than to say anything and waited for her to continue.

"The half-light transforms this room, so that even ordinary spaces take on an unexpected meaning. Look, there is a reindeer pulling a sled and the sorcerer's hat is above it. Where is he? Why did he make himself invisible? Is he hiding because he carries a small child under his coat? A girl whom he rescued? Perhaps from the evil spirits who were planning to destroy the world?"

She would then gesture to the other wall. "Do you see the castle in the clouds? That is probably where he will take her until he is sure that she is safe, and then he will find her parents. He will have a long journey and will probably have to fight many other evil spirits, but he will succeed in defeating all evil. He will achieve all that because with all his heart he believes he knows how and that he can—and you know that is a very special power and requires imagination, right?"

On other occasions, she would make up a story that involved another little girl who found herself in a very scary situation, but would be rescued by one of the other characters. A battle or two with evil spirits, or a witch or goblin would always take place before the rescue. But no matter what, no matter how hopeless it seemed, in the end, the girl would be magically transported to a place she imagined would make her safe and comfortable, her castle in the sky.

Each morning, following our story night, and before getting up, I would lie in my bed and watch the rowan tree that grew outside my window. It was not a very big tree, but it was covered in white flowers in Spring and red berries in Summer and Autumn. It was lovely and very special to me. When I was little Mom called it a Tree of Life, and told me that, long ago, it had been a magical tree—it protected children from malevolent beings.

Evil witches, ghosts, dark shadows, and anything that could frighten little children, would immediately lose their might in the presence of the tree's power. The tree was also home to fairies who looked like ordinary birds feeding on the red berries, but whose real purpose was to protect children from any villains that might roam the town during the day or night.

Mom told such stories not just to me, but also to my friends. Whether in the kitchen as she fed us her homemade delicacies, or on sleepovers, she would spin tales around us all as we watched, entranced. I suspect they wanted to come over so often because they hoped that she would create a new one for them. They would later tell me how much they envied me for having such a cool Mom. We were very young, but even then we all could see that she was different and in no way resembled the other Mothers.

She was never sad, she read voraciously and could quote lines from books, could hum any melody after hearing it only once and recognized every false note. She loved opera and often sang arias from her favorites to me. But, what I loved most about her was her vivid imagination. To this day, I think of it as her most endearing quality. I think she did too, since she seemed to thrive on storytelling and turned any event she witnessed, or even just heard about, into a fascinating tale worthy of a movie. All my friends agreed.

When we were about ten or eleven, and no longer believed in fairies, Mom easily convinced us all that although fairy tales were indeed just beautiful fantasies, magic spirits did exist. In a way that only she could, filled with passion, she told us they were present in the souls of people who were creative, strong-willed, and, most importantly, in those who possessed a powerful imagination. She would repeat this many times, always stressing that this particular gift enabled such people to change anything at will.

Years later, that same imagination would begin to tear us apart, and no matter how much better than facts these inventive narratives sounded, it was hard for me to accept them, when they were lies. But, as a child, you never doubt your mother, or suspect that your parents might have moved somewhere to escape something; that there may be secrets, dark things, hidden in their past. I could not see the dissonance between that fantastical imagination and the reality of her existence. She was my magical mother, I adored her, and, of course, believed everything she ever told me. And, more than anything, I wanted to be just like her.

A Castle in the Sky for Christmas

It was the day before Christmas Eve, sometime after we moved to Wałbrzych, around 1952. Though we did not celebrate that holiday, my mother invited guests for a festive dinner the next day, as she had done for as long as I could remember. That afternoon, she was already done with baking, and the house was filled with aromas of the elaborate three-layer poppyseed cake, the apple strudel filled with cinnamon and raisins, and the Napoleon torte she baked early that morning. The Holiday Tree, as my mother called it, added a fresh and spicy fragrance of its own. The cotton wool served as snow, and the sparkling ornaments, which my mother claimed that she collected for "their artistic" value, further enhanced the already festive atmosphere.

As Mom was busy preparing her shopping list, I felt it would not hurt to remind her, just one more time (for at least the eleventh time in the past hour), to bring some extra money for marzipans. This exotic sweet was available only at this time of the year, and only if one had enough money to bribe the salesperson to bring it out from "under the counter" of our town's only deli, where all delicacies were kept for the black market customers. With a wink and a conspiratorial smile Mom went to Daddy and asked so I could hear, "Would you please give me lots of 'extra' money so I can buy the coveted treat your darling girl wants so much?"

By the time we finally left the house, it was very cold and the snow was coming down hard, but when Mom suggested we walk instead of taking the tram, I felt a familiar excitement. A trip through the park with my mother always meant an adventure in fairyland! As soon as we left our building Mom paused and exclaimed "Look around you and see why I always say that nature is the most creative artist."

Covered in the white, sparkling snow, the usually dirty streets and the gray old buildings looked so different! Gone was the grime and soot, and the scenery that appeared before my eyes could have passed for a picture from my book of Christian Andersen fairytales! As we entered the park, one that I crossed every day on my way to school, the sun peeked out and Mom took my hand as she whispered "let your imagination take over now. We have just entered a land of magic!"

The top branches of the leafless trees, gnarled and foreboding only a few days ago, now bent under the heavy white snow, formed a canopy overhead. As we walked on, Mom whispered "Now we are about to enter a land sprinkled with diamonds."

And it was—sparkling, still and so beautiful! As we walked, holding hands, I could not help thinking how much I cherished those rare times alone with my mom when she wasn't busy playing bridge, reading, or having coffee with her "intellectual" cronies. I kept quiet, hoping that inspired by what was around us, she would make up yet another original take on one of Christian Andersen's fairy tales. That afternoon she told me about a little girl, Emma, whose birthday fell on Christmas day.

Emma, an orphan whose parents died when she was very little, lived with her aunt and uncle and their two spoiled daughters. She was not treated well but she had nowhere else to go. She was not allowed to attend school and, instead, had to do all the chores around the house. Yet, she was not an unhappy child—she had a vivid imagination and every night she met different magical creatures who took her on exciting adventures that always ended in the same beautiful place where her parents were alive and where she lived happily ever after. The only time that she felt very sad was on Christmas Eve, when her aunt and uncle celebrated the holiday with their children while she was in her room all alone.

The Christmas Eve before Emma was to turn eight, her uncle announced that she was old enough to finally do something to earn a living. He handed her a big box of matches and in a stern voice said "Do not come back, unless you bring some money with you."

Shivering, in the freezing cold, Emma walked around for a long time offering the matches to anyone who looked her way, but no one seemed interested. She soon got very tired and to warm herself, she lit a match. As she had always done when she felt sad, she imagined herself in a warm and safe place. As the match flared, a beautiful Christmas Tree appeared before her but before she had a chance to really look at it, the match went out and the tree disappeared. She lit another match, closed her eyes, and willed the vision to come back. Soon she found herself in a brightly lit room with the Christmas tree and a table set with a sumptuous holiday feast.

Mesmerized by the sight, Emma lit one match after another in order to keep these visions alive. She was about to light her last match left when she looked up to the starry sky and saw a shooting star. She closed her eyes, and, as dreamers like her often do, she imagined herself being transported to that special safe place where nothing bad ever happened, and food, even raisins and marzipans, were plentiful.

Mom stopped there, and before I had a chance to ask how the story ended, we had reached the deli.

The store was very crowded and we took our place in line. In front of us, a very young girl, skeletally thin, was impatiently tugging on her mother's sleeve as she repeatedly said "Remember, Mommy, you promised to buy me a chocolate."

Kissing her very gently, over and over, the woman quietly explained that she would but only if there was enough money left over after the necessary purchases. The little girl nodded, temporarily satisfied. But as soon as her mother paid for the three slices of ham, one loaf of bread, and a little butter, she lifted her little girl and quickly walked towards the exit. Between sobs, the girl now loudly complained that she did not get the promised treat.

My mother flung all the money from her purse on the counter and, smiling sweetly, asked the salesperson "Would you please hurry and give me six of the biggest chocolate bars, a pound of ham and butter, three pounds of sausages, and a box each of raisins and almonds?"

As soon as the package was handed to her, she pulled my arm and, at a steady trot, rushed away. She did not turn around even when the sales lady called out "Lady, you have some change coming!"

I had no chance to ask for my marzipans. As soon as we started following the woman with her little girl, Mom motioned for me to keep quiet. We did not stop until we saw the mother and daughter enter a building. After a moment, Mom followed, with me in tow. It was very dark inside and the smell of urine was suffocating, but Mom did not seem to notice. We quietly followed them into the basement, where she then dropped the entire bag of shopping by their door. She rapped loudly on the door and we ran back up the stairs. Tugging my arm so hard that we almost fell, she pulled me out of the building.

She would not talk to me on our walk home. I kept looking up at her, expecting some explanation, but something about her demeanor left no doubt I should remain very quiet. When we got home and Daddy asked her if she bought my marzipans, she looked at him with much contempt and responded, "No, I did not. Your precious child has everything she ever dreamt of so, instead, I bought a castle in the sky for another girl"

Both Dad and I were very puzzled, but she would not explain further. With yet another one of those dismissive waves, she angrily remarked that she did not expect us to understand. And we did not. My father was never able to understand that side of her. That particular Christmas, we had neither a goose nor any of the spectacular dishes my father loved and came to expect. But the meal Mom prepared was still delicious and no one noticed that it was not as fancy as usual.

I probably wouldn't have remembered anything about that Christmas Eve, but, some years later, only a few days before we left Poland, a woman I didn't know came bearing goodbye gifts for the whole family. While Mom went to the kitchen to prepare coffee and cake, the woman, Maria, told us how Mom left food anonymously by their door for a long time after one Christmas Eve, many years ago.

"That night, I heard a noise outside the door but could not see who left that package of food. But next week when I heard the knock, I responded quickly and caught sight of Zosia walking away. I called out, invited her in and we were friends ever since. She brought food for the family for many months after, but more importantly, she often came just to tell stories she made up just for my daughter, after she found out that our little Evie had tuberculosis. Evie really liked the fairy tales that ended in a magical place where everyone was happy. She told me that she dreamed every night of being able to see the castle in the sky."

"When my daughter died," Maria said, "I hoped that her dreams came true."

Maria also mentioned that my mother came to the little girl's funeral and that she did not stop bringing food until Maria's husband, who was also sick with tuberculosis, got well enough to work again.

Listening to her, Dad asked Mom why she never mentioned any of it and, for months after we left Poland, I questioned her about it. But whenever I broached that subject, Mom's face took on a strange expression and all she would say was "Maybe one day you'll understand." I am not sure if I did, but nevertheless, I always wanted to be like her and, in that respect, still do.

I always thought of her castles in the sky as wishful thinking, benevolent flights of fantasy, intended only to brighten the lives of those she shared them with. But maybe she built those castles as a place of refuge for herself, or, considering the secret, to hide something else? Or maybe to make up for something? Something she never told me? Has the secret been hidden in the shadow of those castles in the sky, all these years? Or am I letting the fear of the unknown, and the strife of what our relationship became, discolor even those things about my mother that were so good and beautiful?

Pseudo Appendicitis and The Gypsy

When Mom had been diagnosed with lung cancer, I went home to Australia to spend some time with her. As always, she was still carefully made up and dressed in her immaculately tailored clothes, but I noticed she was getting tired often and kept losing weight. We talked a lot, but mostly I listened as more and more she reminisced about Poland. Suddenly recalling the story about Maria and her daughter, I begged her to tell me more.

She looked at me in a very strange way and remarked that perhaps I had finally developed some imagination. Had she really forgotten it? It is interesting how time can play with our memories, some things that we believe we remember clear as day, never really happened at all. Other things are so clouded that we can't be sure if they ever did. Thinking back on that conversation with my mother, I wonder if she even remembered that she had shared some deep secret with Fela, to be told to me only after she died. With the dissonance that surrounds us, and builds up throughout our lives, can we ever really remember anything that is true at all? Will I ever be able to uncover the secret, and if I do, is there any way to know if it is the truth? I am sure that the events of that day before Christmas Eve, and what followed, are not a figment of my imagination, although, when I was very young, I was a pretty good inventor of my own stories.

Prompted by my mother throughout my childhood, I kept practicing and kept on convincing myself that if I wished hard enough, anything I desperately wanted would eventually come true. The one thing that I always dreamed of, more than anything in the world, was a sibling, and especially a brother. Yet, no matter how much I wished for one, I remained an only child. I hated it because I often felt very lonely. No siblings, or loving grandparents, uncles, aunts, or cousins! And, my parents went out a lot, leaving me alone. Then I usually cried myself to sleep.

One day, when I felt particularly sad and alone, I decided to build my own magical secret world in the niche behind the piano in our living room. Here, my doll became my baby brother and my stuffed animal a special dog, a faithful pet that I named Amik, short for Amicis, the author of my favorite children's story "The Heart." At first, I never mentioned my new brother and pet to anyone. But when my friend came to visit a few days later, I told her that I now had a sibling and a dog. When she insisted on seeing them, I told her that if any stranger goes in to see them, or even talks about them, he or she would be turned to stone. She never asked again.

In fourth grade, I was called out in class to read aloud an essay I was assigned for my homework. I had completely forgotten to do the assignment, but I loved the book we were supposed to write about, and knew exactly what I would have written. I got up and confidently walked to the podium holding my notebook and easily ad-libbed as I pretended to read it.

The teacher suddenly stopped me "I don't think you wrote this by yourself, someone must have helped you."

"Of course I wrote this all by myself," I said.

"No, stop lying to me! I am sure you cheated, let me see your notebook"

She was aghast when she saw the empty pages.

"I knew that you lied," she continued, angrily "Sit down and I will deal with you later"

I could not understand and kept repeating

"I am not a liar and I did not cheat!"

When I came home and related the incident to my mother, she thought the whole matter was hilarious. With that dismissive wave of her hand, she told me "Forget it, and do not give it another thought. Mrs. K is yet another one of those unfortunate people who cannot relate to the wonders of creativity."

I did not know it at the time, but a few years later Mom told me that the next day she went to confront Mrs. K. They argued fiercely and my mother told Mrs. K. that her daughter was already a good writer. She dismissed Mrs. K's. every concern with a wave of her hand and walked away, but not before telling Mrs. K. that even if I did not write it down in my notebook, I did my homework. That being creative and having the ability to make things up is a talent that can occasionally even save lives! I guess she did manage to convince Mrs. K of that.

From that day on, I became that teacher's favorite student. Is it any wonder that I continued making things up?

A year later, my best friend, Ida, was called up to the blackboard to demonstrate how to solve a math problem we were assigned as homework. Instead of working on it, she and I read Anne of Green Gables, the new book my father bought for me. How could a math problem ever compare to the exploits of Anne and Gilbert? Ida had always been an exemplary student, but now she stood silently in front of the whole class, with no idea what to do! When I saw the pained look on her face, I knew she was counting on me to help her, but I didn't know how to solve the problem either!

Clutching my stomach, I began crying and begged my teacher to take me to the hospital. I screamed in pain when the school nurse touched my tummy and, convinced that I was in danger, she transported me to the nearest hospital. I was terrified of the trouble I would be in if I confessed that there was nothing wrong with me, so I continued screaming every time a nurse or the doctor attempted to examine my stomach. Diagnosed with an inflamed appendix, I was operated on right away.

I never confessed any of this to my parents or anyone else. It remained a secret between Ida and me, and it was soon forgotten. Our friendship continued even after I left Poland and we stayed in touch and even saw each other a few times. We always had a lot in common, but nothing was ever as entertaining as when she reminded me of my "creative" moments.

She once asked me, "Having a mother like you had, how did you manage to become such a normal person?"

That question, filled with so many implications, surprised me, but I was not ready to discuss this with anyone, so I quickly replied "Never mind that! Aren't you glad that she brought up a child who would sacrifice her appendix to spare her best buddy punishment and humiliation?"

Once again, we laughed and hugged and then tried to think of other great stories about my mother. She asked "Do you remember the Gypsy?" I smiled at the memory, how could I forget the gypsy?

One summer, Mom and I stayed in a fashionable resort closer to our hometown, instead of going to our usual hotel on the Baltic coast. The weather that day had been sunny and windy, too cool for the pool, but too nice to stay inside. When Mom's bridge game was canceled, she quickly became bored and restless. After rummaging through her suitcase, Mom found a colorful kerchief to cover her long blond hair. Next, with the help of a needle and thread, she transformed two short skirts into one long, tiered one. A white peasant blouse with colorful embroidery, some makeup, and many long necklaces completed the outfit. Next, she borrowed a deck of cards from the front desk of the hotel. She was a gypsy now, she told me, and under no circumstances was I to say otherwise. I was to follow behind her, but at a distance, and could not talk to her no matter what.

The first couple she approached shooed her away, but a lone woman sitting on a bench put out her hand and allowed Mom to read it. She must have been satisfied with what she heard because she agreed to have her fortunes read from the deck of cards my mom held out. After a few minutes, the woman was beaming, then laughing loudly, and, as she walked away, she told every person she passed how funny and surprisingly clever the gypsy was. Before Mom had a chance to leave, another woman asked if she could have her fortune told. She, too, was delighted with what she heard and was singing the Gypsy's praises as she went away.

And then they just kept coming and pushing money in Mom's hand, even though she refused every time. I was bored but Mom didn't seem to notice, so I wondered about looking for something to do. Before I knew it, I was lost. Looking for someone to help me, I spotted a woman I saw at breakfast in our hotel every day and asked her to please take me back to the hotel. She asked a lot of questions and mumbled something about an irresponsible parent, but grudgingly walked me back. As we neared the hotel, I spotted my mother and ran towards her waving my hand. But Mom either did not see me or pretended not to, so I thanked the lady and told her that I would join my mother.

As soon as the lady turned her back, I walked towards Mom, but sat a couple of benches away, waiting for her to finish whatever she was doing. The old couple talking with her seemed deeply engrossed. This went on for what seemed like forever, and when she finally got up to leave, I silently followed, just as I had been told. Away from the crowds, she slowed down and let me catch up to her. That evening, she told me I could stay up late!

When she appeared in the dining room in her gypsy garb, sans the headscarf, the first woman whose fortune she told, recognized her immediately. She was obviously upset when she approached us and, in a shaking voice, asked why Mom pretended to be a Gypsy and willfully gave her false hope?

"What do you mean false hope?" Mom asked, loud enough for everyone to hear "Even though I am not a Gypsy, and might not be able to tell the future like they do, I assure you that if you believe what I told you, but only if you do, everything I promised you, will come true."

Soon the room was vibrating with excited whispers, followed by laughter, and then an applause that was deafening. Mom spent the night being toasted and for days continued to be praised whenever we showed up for dinner. But I wanted to know why Mom had lied to that poor woman.

"Lie?" she asked, "I did not lie. I told her something she so obviously wanted to hear and that made her happy."

"Besides," she said, "and remember it always—if you desire something fervently and you can imagine what it would be like, believe it is possible, that wish will come true. If this woman chooses to believe me, her wish, too, will be granted"

When we went back to that resort the following summer, that same woman kissed my mother's hand and cried happily when she loudly announced that the prediction had indeed come true. She must have told many of the guests at the hotel about it, for I heard whispers that Mom, despite not being a gypsy, possessed the "gift." The gypsy story became a little different, more elaborate, and exciting each time I heard it over the many years Mom shared it, but she never revealed what she told that woman and it did not matter one bit to me. Knowing that the woman's wish did come true convinced me that passionately believing something is possible, will make it happen.

Soon after, however, I would begin to have serious doubts that just wishing for something could make it happen. One summer, my mother unceremoniously left me and my father, and we had no idea when, or if, she would come back. I sincerely and most fervently wished, every evening and every morning, that she would change her mind and appear in my room in the morning. Not only did my wishing not summon her back to me but soon after I was abandoned again, this time by the only other person who loved me. Is it possible that the key to the secret lies in that mysterious absence?

While it was a nice thought, that you can make anything you want happen if you wish hard enough, it was also a dangerous one. I will never know if my mother really believed this, or if she was just trying to make the people around her feel better. Compared to the grim world that she had survived, the idea that all of your wishes could come true was surely seductive. Or, maybe, she believed it because she had been saved, against all odds. I am pretty sure that there are no clues to the secret to be found in my mother's adventure as a gypsy. But then why do I feel doubt? Why do I feel the need to scrutinize every episode, every conversation, for a hint of something that I was never meant to know?

A New Bicycle and a Downward Spiral of Speculation

The winter before I was abandoned, for my tenth birthday, my father surprised me with a brand new bicycle. Even though he was eager to teach me, we had to wait until late Spring to practice. I was a coward, and truly terrified when we first took it out. Every day, as soon as he came home from work, Dad spent an hour or so running behind me while holding onto the bike, and saying over and over "You can, I know you can!"

But even after a few days of that, I was still too scared and begged him not to let go. He put his arms around me and said, "When you start pedaling, I am going to be quiet, but you say out loud 'I know I can, I know I can!' Listen to your voice only, and nothing else"

I did as I was told, and did not even realize that he was no longer holding onto me. Dad whooped, kissed me, and said "Do this any time you think you cannot do it—you will soon see that you can, but first, you must believe in yourself. I know you well and I'm sure that you can conquer any of your fears and reach any goal you set for yourself."

But, although I would never have admitted it to him, it took me a long time to be confident enough to enjoy riding the bike by myself. When I finally did and decided to ride it every week to my piano lesson, I was hit by a drunk riding a motorcycle. I must have fallen hard because I don't even remember how I ended up in the hospital—there were no cell phones, and, where we lived, certainly no car drivers to pick me up. But I do remember that I had a cast on before my mother got there. My right arm was broken in two places and the plaster covered me from the waist up to my shoulder!

As luck would have it, it was the hottest June on record, and I was soon sweating profusely and itching so badly that I resorted to shoving knitting needles inside to scratch. When I began to smell, I kept pouring Mom's perfume inside the cast. I had painful blisters, Mom was furious with me, the sting was unbearable and I felt miserable. But that misery paled in comparison to how I felt when Mom announced that she was leaving for Israel. Summer vacation had just started and

I could not believe that she would abandon me when I was so uncomfortable. I begged, I cajoled and cried, but to no avail. She and our neighbor Julian were going to "explore the country where palms and oranges grew in the desert, where there was no winter and the sun always shone brightly all year long"

I had always suspected that Julian was far more than just a 'neighbor' to my mom and this seemed to confirm it. Why else would she be going with Julian and not with me and Daddy? Each time I asked, she just smiled, and said, "Don't worry, Daddy will take good care of you."

She did not hug me, and there were no kisses to comfort me. A few days later, when I woke up, Daddy was making my breakfast. Mom and Julian were gone. As the days passed, Daddy became increasingly despondent. After her departure he would sit by the phone (there were not too many of those in our neighborhood), waiting for some news from Mom, but she never called and we both cried a lot. I became inconsolable. We would go out for dinner every night, and Dad let me order whatever I wanted. He often invited my friends to join us and tried his hardest to comfort and entertain me. But no matter how hard he tried, my tears did not cease. I cried endlessly, especially every morning when it was time for me to go to school and Dad to work.

At night, I made up stories in which my mother was kidnapped by fairies and brought back home to me on a magic carpet. But it did not help. I was miserable. I was allowed to stay up late and Dad tucked me in every night, but as he was leaving, I would cry "I want Mommy to come back." Dad often stayed in my bed, late into the night, until I fell asleep. I was sure Mom was never coming back, that she left because I complained too much and maybe was mad at Daddy for spoiling me, and she decided she loved Julian more than she loved us, and would stay with him in Israel. I never mentioned those fears because I couldn't bear to make Daddy feel even worse.

I think such thoughts crossed Dad's mind as well, for he became more and more subdued, as more time went by. Were we both right? Had they planned to escape? Mom was gone about a month when Daddy announced that he had a surprise for me.

"You know how you always want to do things all by yourself and we always tell you that you are not big enough? Well, guess what—I just bought a train ticket and you're going on the train, all alone, to visit your "aunt" Hana in Gliwice, your birthplace! You always asked when you could do that and I think that now you are old and mature enough"

At any other time, I would have jumped with joy but, at that moment, all I could think was that Daddy was abandoning me now too, just like Mom. He was giving me away to these people, who were not even real relatives, and my pretend "aunt" Hana was now to become my new mother. But I just nodded my head. Hana and her husband Ziggy adored me. They were childless, spoiled me rotten, and fed me all my favorite sweets, and my father called every night. But no amount of sweets and phone calls could make me happy again. I kept blaming myself for making Mom run away. I knew that it was my fault. I complained so much about my injury, that I drove Mom out of Poland. And, then, I cried so much after she was gone that Daddy too, could not stand me anymore. It was hardly surprising that they had given me away to some fake relatives. Soon I convinced myself that I would never see my parents again. The one photo I have from that visit, shows a sad, chubby child, holding a telephone in her hand.

But, after three weeks, Daddy did pick me up, and, to our surprise, Mom came back soon after. Deep down, I never forgave her for leaving us, but also never stopped feeling guilty. Despite my residual feelings, everything seemed to simply go back to the way it had always been, but I was not the same and neither was my parents' relationship with Julian. Shortly after my mother's miraculous return, Daddy and Julian had a huge fight.

Julian and his wife and daughter lived in the same building as we did and often just dropped by. He was always welcome and was usually invited to have a drink, or dessert, or even just coffee. But the first time he stopped by after their return from Israel, Daddy took Julian into the kitchen with him and closed the door. Mom stayed with me and seemed very nervous, especially when we heard Daddy and Julian screaming at each other. This lasted for a while and then Julian left, slamming the door behind him. Mom sent me to bed—there was no bedtime story, no kiss and even Daddy did not come to say goodnight.

Julian and his wife Dora never visited us again. My father began to take many more business trips, never missed a soccer match, and brought me for rides on his motorcycle almost every Sunday. We would sneak out in the morning when Mom was still asleep. On the back of his motorcycle, holding on tight to him, with my hair blowing in the wind, I was the happiest kid on earth. He would go slowly at first, but, then, increasing the speed and, screaming "Hold on tight," he would tilt the motorcycle almost to the ground. We both whooped and hollered and I laughed so hard that tears would flow down my face.

Daddy seemed more relaxed and eventually was back to his usual calm self, possibly because, one day, Julian and Dora just disappeared from our lives. All of their friends and neighbors were puzzled but, after a while, Mom told them all that she heard from her friend who lived in Germany that Julian had moved his family there. Soon enough, Julian was simply another one of my mother's stories, but the story never mentioned anything about their mysterious time in Israel. If Julian ever came up in conversation, or my mother felt the need to demonstrate the fickleness of life, she would tell a story about a painting:

"In 1954, together with Julian and Dora, we took a short vacation by the sea. We rented a small house from a fisherman and his wife. As soon as Julian walked into his bedroom, he became fascinated by a large painting of flowers hanging over the bed. I could not understand what attracted him to that particular painting, for it was pure kitsch. The colors were gaudy, the flowers clumsy and there was nothing remotely attractive about it. Even the frame was amateurish.

But Julian loved the picture, and, a day before we were all to leave, approached the homeowners and asked if he could buy it. The husband was eager to sell, but his shrewd wife, sensing an anxious buyer, resisted, claiming it was her favorite item in the house. Julian smiled, told her he understood, and dropped the subject. As the group was saying goodbye to the owners, the woman, realizing she had lost an opportunity to make some money, suggested that if Julian would be willing to pay just a little more, she might agree to part with her lovely painting. Julian played hard to get for a little while, but then graciously agreed.

The framed purchase was rather awkward to carry, but when I suggested that it might be wise to take the picture out of the frame, roll it up and leave the frame behind, Julian laughed. Pointing to the headless nails on the frame, he whispered 'the frame alone is probably worth a lot of money.'

On the train back home, he took great care not to leave the painting out of his sight even for a minute. And yet, to my great surprise, Julian never hung the picture in his house and refused to address the question as to why he did not. After Julian moved to Germany, he brought the painting to an auction house. They confirmed that the frame was very old but they also informed Julian that he was right when he suspected that there was another painting underneath the gaudy flowers. In fact, they were able to verify that it was a genuine Titian, a leading painter of 16th-century Venice. Julian agreed to have it sold at an auction and it fetched about a million dollars.

He used the money to purchase a sports Mercedes, a car he had dreamed of for many years! He also bought a beautiful house in Germany and a luxurious villa on the Amalfi coast where he intended to retire. Unfortunately, the first time he drove his precious sports car from Germany to Italy, he was swiped off the road by a huge bus and died instantly."

It remained one of her favorite stories to tell late into her life. Could there be some connection between that mysterious absence, the secret, and Julian's painting? Maybe she and Julian had planned to go to Israel, sell the painting, and stay together, but could not find any buyers and were forced to come back. It is plausible that Mom might have shared all this with Fela, her friend in Israel, who had alerted me to the existence of the secret. Could Fela have even been witness to their escapades in Israel?

If my mother's secret was something as simple as an illicit affair and failed plans to leave us, it would actually be a relief. Such a reality seems almost quaint compared to the other garish scenarios that have been playing in my mind for so long now. Compared to the horrors I have dreamed up, a simple affair would be so insignificant. But, as with anything my mother said, her story about Julian and his painting must be taken with a certain skepticism: I have no idea if any of it is even true. Maybe, the entire story itself is nothing more than a smokescreen. After all Julian and his family disappeared in mysterious circumstances, with only my mother's word accounting for what became of them.

Dwelling on the secret too much makes me very suspicious and, probably, paranoid. I keep inventing theories that swell in my mind and I cannot ignore them. I wonder what Fela would think if she knew the spiral that her revelation, and later withholding, had sent me on. Would she still have decided that not sharing the secret with me was for my own good, if she knew how it would haunt me?

Maybe I am the daughter of Lyev, the Russian soldier who had helped my mother, or maybe, even, Dr. Schmidt, the German doctor who saved her, is my real father. Or, maybe I was mistaken all along and it had actually to do with my father and not my mother. His past is as equally shrouded in mystery as my mother's. The more possibilities I thought of, the more overwhelmed I became. It soon became too much to keep to myself, and I started to share my theories with some of my family. Their reactions to my outlandish theories ranged from aghast to bemused. I cursed my vivid imagination when I saw their expressions, particularly when I saw the look on my daughter's face after I shared my speculations with her.

All three children gently pointed out, several times, that a simple DNA would reassure me, and rule out at least a few of my theories. I knew they were right, but instead of just doing the test, I kept theorizing, agonizing and postulating my own ideas of what the secret held. I must admit, at times, these theories were completely outrageous fantasies. After bombarding them with more and more elaborate theories for months, it was not surprising when, one day, our oldest son, Ben, very casually mentioned that he had his DNA tested, and that the results showed that he was 98.9 percent Jewish. He said nothing else, but knowing my child, I was sure that he did this to reassure me. The relief I felt was enormous. At least two possibilities—that I might not be Jewish, and that I might be Dr. Schmidt's daughter—were crossed off my list.

Ben did not stop there. Having heard all his life about my mother's vivid imagination and convinced that I, her daughter, was also capable of letting my own imagination go wild, he ordered a DNA kit for me as well. I was elated when my result showed that I am 89.7 percent Jewish, and yet I still couldn't rule out the possibility that I was not my father's child. When I tried to casually mention this doubt to Ben. He wasn't the slightest bit fooled by my feigned nonchalance and said "If you're still worried, why don't you ask your brother to have his DNA checked too? If you share 50% of your genes, at least you'll stop worrying about not being your father's daughter."

When I asked my brother to have his DNA tested, he laughed "Why are you so obsessed with the secret? What difference does it make? At your age? Why bother? You are 72 years old —how would this change anything at all? Will you love me any less if I am not technically your brother? Please tell me what is so important about this? Let me try to understand"

I had no words that could explain it to him. Was my family right? Should some secrets be allowed to fade away? I knew for certain that nothing could change my fond childhood memories of shared joy and experiences with my father and mother. And that I loved and admired her despite being terribly irritated by some of her traits. Her many talents, especially the ability to make any event she witnessed so much more interesting than it actually had been, never ceased to amaze me even when her invented narratives made me so angry that I could not be around her for longer than a couple of hours. But perhaps that was not obvious enough to her? Maybe I was too irritable with her and too often. Too harsh. If only I could have been more understanding, more tolerant. Did she feel abandoned by me? I could have been more patient and certainly more tolerant, and the guilt that I feel is immense. After all, she was my mother.

The Cost of Luxury in Communist Poland

Why am I convinced that the secret is my mother's alone? It is possible that I have let my mother's flaws, and the dread of this unknown secret, poison my memories of her, while inflating my love for my father. But, I am convinced that I am not letting some starry-eyed vision of my father cloud my judgment. I recognize that he was not perfect and that there are many things that I do not know about my father. But the things I don't know about him never felt like secrets, and still do not. Even as a child, I knew about his dealings with and feelings about the communists.

I distinctly remember how, right after Stalin's death, he told me how much he despised him and his politics, and how the upper echelon of the Party shamelessly lived like monarchy while preaching equality to the impoverished Polish workers. But Dad had a survival instinct and knew how to circumvent that system. When the war was over, he became friends with many Russian officers, especially those who had easy access to smuggled goods.

Through his connections with Lycv, the soldier who had rescued my mother and took part in their wedding, he made black market connections that he used to obtain illegal goods both for ourselves and our neighbors, who were more than happy to pay for luxury items that they couldn't get in the ordinary store. Those connections continued to be of help, even after the Russians had left Poland and Dad moved his family to Wałbrzych. After a short stint as a barber, he was hired to manage the only department store in our town, and was once again in a position to sell smuggled goods "under the counter."

It was a dangerous feat, but, as he said "If our leaders can have nice clothes, stockings or shoes, all because they have connections to the Russian's, why shouldn't our people? And since I have such contacts as well, why shouldn't I use them to get such goods for us and our neighbors? I'm not pretending to myself or anyone else or that I'm not doing it for profit, but I'm also not stealing from anyone and not forcing anyone to buy from me, so it is a win-win for all." He would often gleefully remark "I can honestly say that I am doing nothing but dutifully following the example of those hypocrites up at the top. Now our family, the commoners, can live as comfortably as they do."

Fashionable clothes were the most profitable goods, some smuggled from Germany, some from Czechoslovakia, others handmade made by the same Polish seamstress the Party members used. There were also handmade shoes, silk stockings, and Russian perfumes. It turned out that all these transactions were far more lucrative than Dad could ever have imagined. Mom and I were well dressed and we could all vacation in the same expensive resorts as the people at the top, and Dad had more opportunities to make even more valuable connections. Soon we had a telephone and a cleaning woman, unthinkable extravagances for ordinary Polish citizens. We also somehow had access to hard-to-get books and, by 1956, we were one of the first families in our neighborhood to own a television set and a washing machine! My father had a motorcycle and, for a short time, a car with a driver. We even owned a tape recorder! The very height of technology at the time. All this came at a great price, however.

One evening, in December 1960, there was a knock on the door and four men walked in. Without any explanation, they began to search the apartment, ripping apart books and tossing everything out of every closet. It didn't take them long to find some of the stacks of money that my father had hidden away in the house. He was cuffed and dragged off without any further explanation. When my mother went to the police station the next day, she was told that he had been transported to Łódź. The official smugly added "Since your husband has no special connections in Łódź, he will be tried and sentenced there. Not here, where he has everyone in his pocket."

Mom spent the rest of the day on the phone. A couple of days later, she packed one small suitcase with a few items of clothing and filled another with money. I was not allowed to go with her, as I was only 14 at the time. She left me with my friend's family, and set off for Łódź, where my father was to be held until his trial.

What happened in Łódź, I only know from my mother's account, but Dad was home soon after her visit to Łódź and always said that it was only thanks to Mom.

This is how she told it.

"After making extensive inquiries (I had a couple of friends in that city, one, a prosecutor), I learned that the judge presiding over your father's trial was fond of beautiful women, liked to indulge in a drink, especially expensive liquor, and lived a life far above his position, and, thus, was not averse to "tokens of appreciation.""

As soon as I heard all that, I knew I would be able to "handle" him. It helped that he was very handsome and charming. As soon as I walked in, I presented him with a bottle of good French cognac, a small token of appreciation for squeezing me into his very tight schedule. We talked about France and French culture and soon discovered we both loved Molière and Flaubert and that we both enjoyed reading Jules Verne to our children. But, just as I was convinced that I had him wrapped around my finger, and I was about to start negotiating my husband's release, I noticed a little red light blinking behind the judge's desk. The tape recorder we had at home had just such a light when it was recording, so suspecting that the judge was probably trying to trap me by having the conversation recorded, I quickly switched gears. I thanked him profusely for taking the time to see me, and politely asked if he could please explain the charges against my husband, and whether there was any possibility of visiting him that day, or the next.

The judge was so obviously taken aback by the change in tone, that I decided to take advantage of his confusion. Politely, but firmly I pressed for permission to visit, at the same time praising his total professionalism. When he arranged for me to see my husband the following day, I got up, shook his hand, and casually mentioned that the cognac had been, in fact, sent by their mutual friend, and was not to be construed as a gift from me. I walked out, moving my body in the most provocative manner I could muster. I was very shaken by the whole experience and, instead of taking a tram, decided to splurge on a taxi to take me back to my friend's house. The driver talked all the way and I could not wait to get out of the car. When my friend opened the door, the first thing I did was to ask for a stiff drink, and then I screamed "I was in such a hurry to leave that blubber-mouthed taxi driver, that I left the bag with all the money in his car!"

I was inconsolable. I was still crying an hour later when there was a knock on the door. My friend opened it and there was the taxi driver with my bag in his hand.

"So sorry," he apologized "but it took me a while before I realized that there was a bag in the back seat, and another half hour to knock on all the doors in the apartment building, looking for the beautiful, very sad blond."

I hugged and kissed him and invited him to have a drink with us, which he did gladly. During the course of the celebration, it somehow came out that he was Jewish and had lived in the same town as my husband before the war. He knew him from school! When I told him about the incident with the judge, he told me that he "knew some people" and could introduce me to a prosecutor who would be willing to "work" with me. He did just that. The prosecutor was indeed more than willing to "help" and did not have a tape recorder. Once I paid him all the money I brought and promised a little more later, the formalities were quickly concluded, and my husband was transported back to Wałbrzych a week later. All the charges against him were dropped and not too long after we obtained permission to leave the country."

What better proof could I have had as a child that my parents' marriage was perfect and life would always be beautiful? There was nothing that magical mom could not take care of.

Could some hint to the secret lie in my father's incarceration in Łódź, and my mother's adventures in securing his freedom? It is conceivable that something else happened in Łódź that led to my father's freedom and our subsequent escape to Australia, and that the story of the judge and the "blubber-mouthed" taxi driver was yet another distraction. Another witty tale of my mother's to make me believe that everything would always be alright. With such stories filling my everyday existence, is it any wonder I never noticed that perhaps my own life was not always as perfect as I thought?

Just a couple of months before my fifteenth birthday, my parents informed me that we were moving to Australia. The announcement came as somewhat of a shock. While they had been talking about leaving Poland for a few months, no concrete plans had ever been discussed in my presence, so I suspect that my father's arrest had led to the escalation of their plans. As the packing began, Mom told me a lot about Australia. There, koalas hang from every tree and kangaroos graze freely on the lawns, the weather is mild all year round, and enormous beautiful homes line the streets. It all sounded very intriguing, and since the plan also included an extended stay in Italy, it didn't take long before I became excited at the prospect of traveling and even living outside of Poland. At almost fifteen, secure and sheltered, the thought that my life might undergo some major changes did not even enter my mind.

After six very exciting weeks in Italy, followed by three weeks of constantly throwing up aboard the cruise ship "Orcades," we finally arrived in Melbourne. We were met there by Mom's two high school friends, Marta and Erna, who were our sponsors in Australia. With them, I explored Melbourne and the surrounding areas and, to their delight, I was constantly overwhelmed by the wonder of that town. Downtown, or The City, as the residents referred to it, was not as big as I had imagined, but it was nevertheless impressive.

I especially liked the red brick and golden cream stucco building of the Edwardian Flinders Street Station. Stretching for more than a city block, it had grand archways and an expansive ballroom inside. I would take the train as often as I could just to arrive at the station and then stand for a long time on the wide steps, as hundreds of Melbourne residents did every day. Someone told me that the station was a meeting place for businessmen and lovers alike, and I hoped that one day I would find myself there with my one and only.

I spent three whole days exploring the Royal Botanical Gardens, with its picturesque setting extending over 30 or so acres, displaying over 50,000 diverse and exotic plants I had never heard of. The gardens were an easy tram ride from our house, near the center of Melbourne, on the south bank of the Yarra River, where I could imagine myself one day rowing a small boat. As I walked around the campus of Melbourne University, crowded with all those well-dressed young men and women, I dreamt of being a student there in just a couple of years.

I woke up every morning grateful that my parents decided to move here. Australia was so grand and exciting! This was especially true as I rummaged through the many stores that lined the Melbourne streets, all filled to capacity with fashionable dresses, shoes and handbags! In Wałbrzych, there was only one clothing store, and you could rarely find anything more than some drab, ill-fitting clothes! But here, in Melbourne, the abundance was true not just of the downtown area, but of the suburbs as well. I greedily took in every detail and immediately upon returning home, wrote letters to my friends in Poland describing every detail. As I walked the streets of our suburb, I marveled over the single-family houses that far outnumbered the apartment buildings, most framed by well-kept gardens and velvety smooth, manicured lawns. And the kitchens! Modern stoves unlike any I had seen in Poland, refrigerators large enough to hold a whole cow, electric ovens, toasters and other gadgets I couldn't even name! Even the house we lived in, a house owned by a lower-income family forced to rent out two bedrooms to us, modest by Australian standards, had many such features.

I will never forget my first visit to Victoria Market! The cornucopia of unfamiliar names was overwhelming as was the noise and the crowds, and the smell and the vibrant colors forced my eyes to greedily feast on the abundance of food products I had not seen before. There were so many stalls filled with fruits I'd only read about in books—pineapples, bananas and passion fruit. My nostrils were constantly bombarded by unfamiliar yet intoxicating aromas of the many herbs and spices in the tiny shops just outside the market. Our hosts delighted in my pleasure and my constant wonder at the omnipresence of stands selling ready to eat products, meat pies, and fried doughnuts. They kept feeding me these delicacies just to see my reaction. Years later, they often recalled, with amusement, the speed at which I consumed these, and the grunts of pleasure I made when I chewed foods that were new to me.

I remember how often I kept saying that Poland was a village compared to this country and that Australia was indeed the paradise my mother promised, even if koalas did not hang from the eucalyptus tree branches and kangaroos did not graze on every lawn. Such small fabrications were, after all, insignificant compared to some others my mother was known for. In my first few weeks in Australia, long before I had ever heard of any secret and without the benefit of hindsight to see the connotations of my father's actions and our self-imposed exile from Poland, it was easy to believe in my mother's vision of a magical world, where anything was possible if you just willed it to be. Little did I know that everything was about to change and my mother's castles in the sky would soon begin to crumble all around us.

New Realities and Old Falsities

I was fifteen years old and about to start a new school in a different country. Though the thought of an all-girl school was rather disheartening, the school's reputation made up for the lack of any potential suitors. I was introduced to the principal of the school, Miss T. an older woman who wore a shapeless grey skirt, which fell well below her knees. Thick stockings of the same color, very practical black shoes, and a shapeless charcoal cardigan completed her wardrobe. There was not a trace of makeup on her face, and her hair, dotted with silver, was pulled back into a severe bun. A pair of steely blue eyes stared right through me as we shook hands. Everything about her demeanor was very proper and stern and screamed supreme authority.

At first, on hearing that I did not understand a word of English, she was averse to even considering my application. But when my mother's friend Marta, one of our sponsors in Australia, appealed on my behalf, whatever she said made Miss T reluctantly agree to have me interviewed by the Literature teacher who was of Polish descent and spoke Polish.

Mrs. W., too, was all business, though there was a sparkle in her green eyes that made her seem far less formidable than Miss T., even when she abruptly cut off my mother's chatter about her brilliant daughter and asked her to leave. Professional, yet sympathetic, she described the tenth-grade curriculum in great detail, and to my utter delight informed me that in tenth grade one could choose between a humanities or a science-based track. I did not have to deal with math anymore! Without a moment's hesitation, I enthusiastically asked Mrs. W. if I could start the next day, even though it meant starting almost in the middle of the year, and skipping a grade.

The interview lasted for another hour and we talked about my interests and my academic performance in Poland, the books I read and liked, my recent travels, and, finally, the career that I hoped to pursue in the future. Excited now, I happily talked about my plans to attend Melbourne University and how I would love to study law. As the meeting concluded, I expressed my deep gratitude for being granted an interview and my sincere hope that I would be accepted. Before Mrs.

W. could say anything, I added quickly that I was eager to learn and would work hard not to embarrass her. Four days later, I donned my school uniform and entered the tenth grade, three months into the school year.

The night before, my mother announced that she, too, had good news. She had already found a job! The three of us had a good laugh as she described the circumstances under which she found her first Australian job. John X, who owned a raincoat factory, took Mom to see Harry W. hoping to convince Harry to employ her in his garment factory. After just a few questions directed at my mother, Harry suggested that perhaps it was John who should be given the honor of employing her. John insisted that the honor should go to Harry.

"After fighting over me," my mother mischievously stated, "John X. capitulated and tomorrow I start working for him, folding raincoats."

My father, too, found employment, he cheerfully announced. His experience of cutting inmates' hair in the concentration camp had turned out to be very useful. The day after he was to begin a career as a barber. Life was going to be good in our new country, we all decided. As we toasted each other with our teacups, not for a moment did we think that the reality we were facing was infinitely different from that idyllic existence we imagined.

For months, every day, and all day long, I was taunted by girls who took exquisite pleasure in making fun of my feeble attempts to speak English. It started on the first day, when I walked into the classroom and, as clearly and politely as I could, said '*haallo*', instead of hello. For weeks later, as soon as I walked through the door of the classroom, the gang of popular girls screamed 'haallo,' imitating my accent and my tone of voice. They laughed even harder when, after working for days on my pronunciation, I greeted them with "*Good day!*" which I thought was more Australian. And it somehow got even worse when, one day, as they kept pointing at me, I heard them call me sheila. Thinking that they had forgotten my name, I walked over and announced "M*y name Anita not Sheila.*" How was I to know that in Australian slang a girl/woman was called sheila? And, of course, the lack of a verb in that sentence gave them even more ammunition for their taunting. But nothing topped the humiliation I felt the day I came to the pool in my old-fashioned bathing suit that looked more like a skirt and sleeveless top than a swimsuit. Giggles, sneers, all kinds of names I did not know at the time followed me for the rest of the school year.

At night, and every night, I watched helplessly as my mother cried and soaked her feet, swollen after a day of standing and folding raincoats in the factory where she now worked. Though my father never complained about anything, he woke up every night screaming from nightmares. Dormant for the past decade, the horrors of Auschwitz had now returned with a vengeance. For the first time in my life, I was scared. My father, the always gentle, patient man, changed. He became more erratic and often lost his patience.

One day when he came home very late from work, he seemed unusually agitated. Mom was listening to Norma and was singing along with Maria Callas and did not react or did not hear when Daddy asked about dinner. Furious, he walked over to the radio, pulled the cord out of the socket, lifted the radio above his head and, thinking he was going to smash it, I screamed. He hesitated just for a second, stopped and then quickly took it out of the kitchen and put it out on the curb by the front door. He went to the bedroom and I did not see him until the following evening. Incidents like that began to happen often. The more Mom ignored him, the angrier he got. And yet, even though he now lost his temper more often, and seemed angry and frustrated almost all the time, he still never lost his patience with me. In fact, throughout my entire life, I remember only two occasions when he did—once, before Mom left us, and then when I was in fifth grade.

It was March 5th, 1953, the day Stalin died, the whole of Poland was in mourning. At our school, teachers told us wonderful stories about him and all, without exception, cried afterward. Weeping crowds filled the streets as I walked home and I too cried uncontrollably when I got home. Dad thought that someone had hurt me.

"Tell me what happened," he asked.

"Daddy, Stalin died, our Djedooshka (Grandfather in Russian) is dead!"

Dad was visibly upset "How many times did I tell you that man was evil? A fake, a hypocrite, and a murderer—stop this nonsense right now!"

He was screaming by now "Daddy, shsh, if someone hears you, you'll go to jail."

I cried even louder and Dad could not calm down, so for the first time in my life, he spanked me really hard. He then hugged me, put me on his lap and carefully explained "All those crying people are rejoicing inside because they all know how terrible that man was, but acknowledging it, means jail or worse. They fake their grief now, afraid that someone is watching, but I bet they all hope that things will finally change now. Don't listen to anyone, including your teachers. Trust me—I would never lie to you. Wipe your nose, wash your face and we will all go out to dinner and instead of crying, we shall celebrate."

I was confused and did not believe him, but I loved him and did not want to disappoint him, so I nodded my head, kissed him, and apologized. Though that had been long before our lives in Australia, I had not seen my father so frustrated since then, and had to remind myself that he was under a lot of stress, and was still my loving Daddy.

But, I could not help thinking about how wonderful my life was before we moved to Australia. We were very comfortable financially, I had everything I ever wanted and, in addition, I had a magical mother who could make life beautiful by making any problem, no matter how insurmountable, disappear with just a wave of her exquisite hand. Where was that mother now that I needed her most? Why, of all times, was she suddenly incapable of waving away our problems? Had that extraordinary mom gone forever and why had she vanished? I arrived home every day to a tired and unhappy woman, who constantly blamed her husband for being unable to provide for us.

To comfort myself, almost every night, I took out my favorite photo of my mother, taken a few years earlier, in Poland: a photo of my mother brushing her long hair in front of a mirror. Even today, I remember that scene very vividly. Daddy brought home an exotic turquoise silk robe from China and Mom put it on, and went to the mirror. The silver dragons embroidered all over the robe, shimmered in the light, competing for attention with her long, shiny platinum blond hair. She was singing her favorite aria from the Merry Widow and seemed particularly happy with her appearance that night. Each stroke of the brush elicited an ever more satisfied smile on her face and I watched awestruck as she stood up to admire the rest of her body. The woman I was looking at was completely preoccupied with admiring herself and at that moment I fervently wished I could be just like her. I always thought her the most beautiful and elegant of all women, but especially so that evening.

When I sensed that we were no longer alone, I turned to see my father snapping pictures with his brand new camera. Mom must have noticed him at the same time, for she proceeded to walk slowly towards him. Something in the way she moved made me want to leave, but before I did, they were on the bed and Daddy was kissing her. Neither seemed aware of my presence. Embarrassed, I left the room very quietly and retreated to my bed, waiting for my mother to give me a goodnight kiss. But that evening she did not come.

Now, in Australia, I looked at that photograph and wondered—what happened to the two people I loved most in the world?

I began to have a recurring dream. An enigmatic creature, waving a scarf embroidered with silver dragons danced in the air to the sound of "One Fine Day" from Madama Butterfly. Mesmerized, I would watch her from my bed. She was so beautiful and so graceful! Sometimes she appeared just for a few seconds as if to tease me and then came back again and again. At other times, she danced for a while and then stretched her arms to me almost as if to say come to me. But whenever I reached for her, she disappeared and I would wake up and not be able to get back to sleep.

I changed. I was constantly overcome by a strange feeling; a persistent, aching sadness, and I refused to see the one friend I just made at school. But, one night, when I woke up from a nightmare feeling particularly sad and depressed, I imagined myself happy, living with my parents in a beautiful house on the rocks by an emerald ocean. Imagining the sound of the waves, I felt better. After that, every evening, before I turned the light off, I would force myself to hear the crashing waves on the rocks just below the windows of our beautiful house. I would look out my window and watch the foam explode into a million stars, and soon I would hear the most beautiful, haunting melody and would then walk down to the white sand beach below our house. My Daddy would join me and when it was time, we would go back to the house where Mom was baking our favorite apple cake while listening to one opera she loved most, Madama Butterfly. She would hug me and embrace Daddy and then they would kiss.

My imagination, dormant for a while now, rescued me again. When I woke up, I could even smell the aroma of the cake and everything around me was beautiful and serene again. I could now build my own castles in the sky! I no longer had any problems sleeping through the night. My Dad's nightmares, however, became even more frequent and now he slept very little. Despite the night terrors and sleep deprivation, he did not give up. He worked even harder and tried his best to cheer us up. He kept telling us that we just needed a little more time, and we were blessed to live in a country that offered so many opportunities.

In addition to his regular job, with permission from our landlord, Zvi, Dad also began to cut hair at home. Zvi soon became a regular. Dad always refused to accept any money from him for his service, and Zvi always got upset. However, after a few arguments, they finally reached an agreement. Instead of payment, Zvi would buy him a lottery ticket and, at Dad's insistence, they would split the prize if they were ever lucky! For months they had much fun speculating what they would do with the money, not for a minute thinking that anything like that would ever happen. What a wonderful shock it was when the impossible did happen and one of those tickets fetched a hefty five-thousand-pound prize, more than either of them had ever dreamed of. This was a whole year's salary for an average person! After sharing the winnings, Zvi paid off his mortgage while Dad used the money to purchase a used car, and buy out his boss at the barbershop. His dream came true and he became a capitalist overnight!

Despite the improvement in my family's finances, I still could not find any joy. Six months after we came to Australia and two months before the end of the school year, life in my new environment was still a constant struggle. My parents fought often and openly, never bothering to lower their voices, or worry that I might overhear. As the atmosphere at home became increasingly oppressive, I began to lose all self-confidence. Even though I had managed to make a couple of girlfriends by then, only one attended the same school and was in a different classroom.

At the time, my English was at least starting to get better. I loved the sound of the language and from the moment I started school I listened intently and sat for hours in front of the television practicing the phrases I heard. Luckily, I had a good ear and picked up the language quickly. My improved language skills were little solace, however; even though I could understand almost everything at school and had been able to pass every test, I still felt very uncomfortable speaking in my new language, terrified that the mean girls at school, who continued to look for any opportunity to make fun of me, would have even more reason to do so.

So, I listened carefully, but rarely engaged my classmates in any conversation, and did not dare take part in any of the discussions in class. Until the day I heard my history teacher, Miss S., one of the teachers I respected and liked a lot, talk about the Molotov–Ribbentrop Pact signed in August 1939. Miss S. described it as a non-aggression pact between the Soviet Union and Nazi Germany, where each pledged to remain neutral in the event that either nation was attacked by a third party; the treaty also included a secret protocol dividing Northern and Eastern Europe between Germany and Soviet Union, anticipating potential "territorial and political rearrangements" of these countries. At first, I thought that I misunderstood something, for, after all, I had covered this part of history in my history lessons in Poland many times. I knew that the Soviet Union and Nazi Germany had been mortal enemies when Germany invaded Poland, on September 1, 1939. The Soviet Union was and always had been Poland's greatest ally.

I listened carefully but could feel the distress of the lies begin to twist my stomach, as Miss S. told the students that Germany and the Soviet Union invaded their respective sides of Poland on September 1, as was agreed, and then proceeded to divide the country between them. How could they believe this? Everyone knew that the Soviet Union was benevolent and peaceful and would never be a party to such unprovoked aggression. I raised my hand and in a shaking voice, full of fear but also indignation, choosing my English words very carefully, I explained that the Soviet Union was, in fact, not an enemy, but a protector of Poland.

This was the first time I spoke in class and I knew that my classmates' sudden attention was caused by the exciting prospect of making fun of my English. Filled with dread and shaking uncontrollably, I quickly sat down and tried hard not to cry. Patiently and slowly, choosing her words so I could understand everything she said, Miss S. began explaining that the official policy of the Soviet Union was to deny the existence of the secret protocol of the Soviet–German Pact, and that the history taught in all countries in the Soviet Block, was, in fact, pure propaganda. She suggested I come to her office after school to discuss this further. The mean girls in my classroom could not have been more delighted at yet another example of my stupidity. Gleefully, they began whispering, pointing at me, and giggling. Although Miss S put an immediate stop to this, they knew they now had rich fodder for further ridicule. And they used it mercilessly for weeks after the incident. But I no longer cared that much, for Miss S. decided to take me under her wing and acted as my protector and mentor from then on. She tutored me not just in history but English as well, though we mainly concentrated on history.

During one of the first tutorials, Miss S. shattered another lie I was taught in Poland. In 1948, Stalin published "Falsifiers in History," a document meant to disprove the publication of the secret protocols and other secret German–Soviet relations documents. In it, Stalin claimed that, during the Pact's operation, he rejected Hitler's claim to share in a division of the world, without mentioning the Soviet offer to join the Axis. I learned that this version, the Stalin version of history, appeared without exception, in all historical studies, all official accounts, as well as memoirs and textbooks published in the Soviet Union and in Poland! It is hard to explain the effect of learning that almost everything you know about your home is a lie, particularly on a young mind.

It seemed as if the only time anyone had told me the truth, had been my father on the day Stalin died. With my reality shaken by the revelation that my own country had lied to me about everything, that conversation with my father so long ago suddenly made more sense. But, looking back, now, thinking about the secret, I wonder, was it only my country that had lied to me? Maybe there is some other reality that I believed in that was just waiting to be shattered. Did I know the real truth about any of my early life in Poland? Am I any closer to the truth, even now?

Miss S. continued to mentor me for the next year and I slowly began to feel confident that I would be able to pass the matriculation exam and realize my dream of attending Melbourne University to study law. For the first time since we arrived in Australia, I was exceedingly happy—all was going well at school, a friend from Poland whom I knew since childhood had just emigrated to Melbourne and came by every day, and I had also made a couple of really good friends.

But despite my happiness and our improved finances, my parents were not at ease. My father's nightmares were more frequent than ever. Though Mom no longer seemed angry, and resembled her old self on the surface, she never missed an opportunity to berate my father. He did not know how to play bridge, was not interested in going to the theater, and he could never understand the needs of a person of her "aristocratic background." When she did not complain about Dad himself, she would inevitably mention how her "dreams were shattered" once she married him. Everything was Dad's fault. He seemed crushed all the time and continually tried to please her even more. He started bringing flowers every Friday and worked overtime whenever possible.

I could not understand what caused their unhappiness. To my teenage mind, things seemed to be going okay. We were not starving and had enough money to live. Our lives were by no means as luxurious as they had been in Poland, but we were okay. Looking back, I wonder if my mother, devoid of the distractions of culture and luxury, could not help but reflect on her own life, on her triumphs and failures, and maybe even her secrets. Perhaps, she did not like what she saw in those reflections, and that drove her to make my father's life as miserable as she herself felt. But, maybe I am being too harsh, again letting the bad feelings of our later relationship, and the shadow of the secret, cloud my judgment. Much as there was a reality in Poland I was unaware of as a child, there is every possibility that there was some other reality, unknown to my teenage self in Australia. It was probably nothing that involved wide-scale propaganda and lying to children en masse, but maybe personal problems or just things that teenagers are not meant to know. I must concede that not every strange action or example of my mother's bad behavior needs to be linked directly to her untold secret.

Another Lie

For the longest time, I thought that the purpose of my imagination was for comfort or to help others. But as time went on, when I was distressed, I built castles in the sky to distract myself from my trouble, just as my mother taught me. However, towards the end of my time in high school, I realized that there were other ways in which my creative mind could be useful, and that castles in the sky were by no means limited to objects of comfort.

One Sunday, Anna, my closest friend at that time, asked me to go with her to a dance. I was very excited! My first social outing! I searched my wardrobe to find something that I could wear. It was summer and pretty hot and I soon realized that I had nothing appropriate. There was no way I could ask my parents for a new dress and my options were to stay home or put on my polka dot dress—though old-fashioned, it was cute enough, I decided. As I entered the dance hall and looked around the room, I became painfully aware that I did not fit in and the same was certainly true of my dress. How could I have accepted the invitation?

I was still not comfortable engaging in a conversation in English. And, I was sure that my pink and white polka dot short sleeve dress was standing out like a sore thumb among the strapless sun dresses the other girls wore. But I was afraid to offend Anna, the girl who stood by me and who insisted I come to this dance, so I stayed. I kept my head down and tried to stay out of her way. I was afraid to look around, in case I caught someone's attention and embarrassed both myself and my friend. But the music was fabulous and I moved to the rhythm, only looking up only from time to time, and that is when I saw him.

He was tall and blond, with piercing blue eyes that locked with mine just as I looked up. I quickly buried my head in my hands terrified that he would see how I blushed. Afraid to look again, I kept my head down and just listened to the happy sounds of people dancing and laughing all around me. I felt like I had to get out of there as quickly as I could. I should not have come, I kept thinking over and over again. Tears were just beginning to form in my eyes when I felt a gentle tug on my shoulder. Afraid to look up, I waited.

"Will you dance with me?" I heard a boy's voice ask in Polish

I was too terrified to lift my head. But I was curious, and when I did, my heart began to pound so hard I almost fainted! Those blue eyes! No, it could not possibly be! He had to have made a mistake! Hesitating, I looked at him and saw those eyes smiling at me.

"I asked if you would like to dance," he repeated quietly.

Before I could answer, his hand reached out for mine and he led me to the dance floor.

"Yes," I answered a little late, afraid to say anything else.

The music was divine, a slow, romantic tango. He slowly spun me around, and then gradually, looking into my eyes, he hugged me closer to him. I felt all tension leaving my body and yet I still could not believe that this was not a dream. We stayed on the dance floor, without speaking, for a long time. He was a terrific dancer and I just wanted everything to go on like this forever. But the music faded away and the musicians started packing up. Please, please, no! This cannot stop yet, I prayed silently.

He asked, again in Polish, "Would you like to take a walk"?

"How did you know?" I asked, embarrassed.

"Oh, your accent, it is unmistakable!"

"Yes." was all I could say.

He smiled and introduced himself, "My name is Janek, what is yours?"

We walked outside. The day had been hot but now there was a cool breeze and although the sky was still blue, pink clouds gently hinted of an imminent sunset. Everything looked more beautiful and peaceful in this light, and even the flowers on my favorite jacaranda trees looked more purple and more attractive than usual. We stood under one when Janek asked if he could kiss me. I had never been kissed before, but at the time I could think of nothing I wanted more. I was afraid and yet so excited!

"I don't know how," I said very quietly without lifting my head.

His lips brushed mine as he gently pulled me to him. The scent of his shaving lotion and the feel of his body pressing into me was scary but simply intoxicating. We kissed for a while, without saying anything at all. Then I realized that Anna must be worried. I did not say goodbye and did not explain. What if she called the police? I panicked and pushed him away. Rushing off, I shouted, "I am sorry but I have to go back!!"

I ran away without saying another word. When I got back to the dance hall, it was empty. There was no sign of my friend and I felt terrible. I called her as soon as I got home and, to my relief, she had seen me leave with Jan, had not worried at all and, in fact, was very excited. She wanted to hear it all and I shared it with her.

"Did he ask you for a phone number?"

Oh, my God, no! With horror, I realized that I would probably never hear from him. How could I have been so stupid? Or, maybe he did not like me enough to ask? Did I not kiss well? Why would a gorgeous guy like him want to go out with me?

A million questions and scenarios flooded my mind. For the next few days, I could think about nothing else. I would not eat and my parents started to worry, but I could not tell them what troubled me. I finally resigned myself to the fact that I was just simply not attractive enough. But the next Saturday morning my father woke me and said "There is a phone call for you. A very polite young man introduced himself, and told me, in Polish, that he is a friend of yours and that he would like to talk to you."

"How did you get my number?' I asked when I picked up the phone.

"Easy. I knew all the people at your table." Oh, the elation!

On the evening of my first date, I went back and forth in front of the mirror, in the new dress that Anna's mother gave me. I talked to myself, I laughed out loud. After that, Janek kept calling every Friday to ask me out. He seemed so nice and sincere and my mother was very impressed when he brought flowers each time he picked me up. My father did not like him for some reason, but would not explain. I wonder if he had seen something in Janek that eluded my mother and me. But, I liked him. He was considerate, gentle and patient and understood that I was not ready for anything more than kissing.

Even after three months of dating, he kept telling me that we could wait until I was ready to get married. He was four years older, had a full-time job piloting a plane that sprayed crops, and kept assuring me that he was in no hurry. I believed him. We dated for a few months when, just before my matriculation exam, he called and asked if I would skip school the next day and meet him in his apartment. I didn't know he had a place of his own!

That morning, I took extra care and glanced in the mirror for the last time. Satisfied with the way I looked, I decided that today was the day I would tell him I no longer want to wait until we got married. When I entered Janek's apartment, he did not hug or kiss me and, instead, suggested we have some sweets and coffee, but I was too nervous to put anything in my mouth. He got up and put on a Platters' record and when I heard it was my favorite 'My Prayer' I thought it was a perfect time to tell him. But, before I could utter a word, he stopped me.

Without looking at me, he quickly blurted out "I am getting married next Saturday."

I listened, but as he continued I became more and more confused. I could not understand and I just wanted to run and get out of there.

"Even though I love YOU" he repeated this several times, "I have been fooling around with Lena"

My friend Lena? The one who always had a boyfriend?

"She is pregnant and I have to take responsibility for my actions, so I am marrying her."

'My Prayer' had just finished and I thought so was my life. I did not want to hear how sorry he was, and certainly not how much he claimed to love me and always would. All I could think was, LIES, always LIES, and more LIES! Am I always going to be surrounded by falsehoods? At school, at home, and here! Am I so naive, so trusting, blind, or simply an idiot? He was so handsome so how could I have thought that anyone like him would want to wait for me?

For the next few days, I could not concentrate on anything else and my schoolwork suffered. Miss S. noticed that something was going on with me. She called me to her office and asked if she could help in any way. I burst out crying but could not tell her.

"These are the last months of year twelve and you have to concentrate on your studies. Your dream is now within your reach, so forget everything else and concentrate on your school work," she said. I knew that if I wanted to go to law school at Melbourne University I could not mess the exams up, no matter what.

The day of the matriculation exam was extremely hot and sitting in the Exhibition Hall, sweat pouring down my face, I began doubting myself. As if they knew what I was thinking, the kookaburras in the trees outside the open windows were laughing mercilessly all the time. But the history exam turned out to be fairly easy, as was Geography. The Literature part of the English exam gave me some problems since I still did not have the vocabulary to express my thoughts in a more sophisticated way, but I knew what I wanted to say and felt I was doing well enough. But when I got to the part 'Clear Thinking', I was suddenly baffled. I thought I understood English, but this was something I just did not get. I read it and re-read it many times, but something was missing and I just had no idea what it was all about. I now know that the questions had little to do with logic but were more about clouded judgment and abstract thinking. But at the time, I just did not get what I needed to do. I was frustrated, and, unable to cope, I left most of that part of the exam blank.

I would not see any of my friends until the results of the exam were posted at the Exhibition Hall and made sure to avoid them all when I went to look. There were no names posted by the results, only numbers that each of us had been issued at the entrance to the exam. At first, I was so nervous that I could not find mine. But there it was:

History—Second Honor. I breathed with relief.

Geography—Second Honor. Hoorah!

Literature—Pass.

Physical Education—Pass.

English—Fail. I gasped with horror.

I was mortified and didn't know what to do. I could not go to university! I tried hard not to cry and did not respond to greetings from my classmates. Instead of going home, I went to the Botanical Gardens and walked for hours. I could not face my mom. Whenever I failed at anything, her comment was always the same, but I knew that today I was not ready to deal with the rage I usually felt for days after.

I finally did go home in the late afternoon, prepared, I thought, not to feel anything at all. But, regardless of what I thought, inevitable feelings of anger and humiliation welled up inside me when she said "Darling, I learn languages much quicker than you, and I could not have passed an English exam at this time either. So don't worry, you'll find a good job, meet a nice boy, you'll get married and have a child. All will be fine, just as it is with me."

Did she not realize that going to University was something I had dreamt of for years? That it was the most important goal I had set for myself?

It was December 1963. I was miserable, had all kinds of nightmares of failing various tests, driving, math and English, all on the same day, and woke up crying every morning. I refused to see my friends, ate a lot of sweets and got fat. It was easy to blame my failure on the trauma of my breakup with Janek. Not wanting to be hurt like that by anyone ever again, I now focused my creative mind on fantasy and stories. My imagination not only helped me sleep at night, but with self-reinvention as well. Using those skills, I had been honing ever since I invented an imaginary brother and pet dog behind our piano in Wałbrzych, I made myself a different person in my mind, and gradually that person began to be reflected in the real world too. The new me was sophisticated and experienced; not one to be taken in so easily by any handsome, sweet-talking, blue-eyed boy. Who better to base this new charming self-assured woman on, but my own charming self-assured mother. I must have been very convincing, for no one doubted any of it. I became very good at turning my own image into what I wanted it to be, at reinventing myself, or, put more simply, inventively lying.

Despite working on becoming a different person, my confident new self still did not really know what to do with her life, so I accepted the first job I was offered. A bank clerk at our local branch—it was terribly boring, but I kept reminding myself that I was now earning a salary and helping my parents. And then, a miracle happened!

Just a month before my 18th birthday, I noticed that my mother and father stopped their whispering as soon as I entered the room. It was so unlike them! I was sure they were plotting something that concerned me, so I asked them right out "Please don't talk about me behind my back—I can handle it, so what are you scheming?"

"Dziubuś, it is not about you at all, your Mom is pregnant!"

At first, I was confused, but Dad reassured me that I heard right. I was going to have a sibling? My elation was soon shattered when they openly started discussing, or, rather, arguing about, abortion. Abortions were illegal in Australia at that time, but Mom was adamant—she was not having a baby at 39. I argued, I begged, and, finally, desperate, I threatened to commit suicide! I tried to explain how I had dreamed all my life about having a sibling. Dad pitched in and suggested that perhaps this was a new start in a new country! I argued that she could not deprive me of a chance to finally have a normal family, that having a sibling would enable me to one day have nieces and nephews and my children, unlike me, would have an uncle or an aunt and, later, cousins! I cried, I screamed, and every night fervently wished that Mom would reconsider. I dreamed about a baby in our house, I threatened again, and, then, I won!

In September 1964, early in the morning, on the day of Yom Kippur, my mother was taken to the hospital—there were some complications, and we were told it would be a long time before they knew what was going on. They sent us home and told us we could not see her for a while. Dad spent the morning in the synagogue, while I, as usual, sat outside it. When we came to the hospital around noon, I was not allowed to see Mom—she was being prepped for a C-section. An hour later my beautiful baby brother entered the world! I was so ecstatic and

75

delighted just looking at the gorgeous little baby, my brother, that I did not worry about Mom. But she was very sick. She had a high fever, some kind of infection and other problems that I did not understand.

I quit my bank job when she finally came home and happily took care of them both for the next few months. Nothing bothered me anymore—I told myself that my baby brother was a far better gift than any boyfriend or a University. Mom was soon on her feet again, and I found a job at the Victoria Education Department as a file clerk. It was only slightly less boring than the bank job, but the people I worked with were very nice and since I did not think that I had any better prospects, I resigned myself to the fate I was dealt.

I soon became distracted by my new place in life, and I had undoubtedly changed. While my newfound, feigned assertiveness did have some benefits, I became so entangled in one particular lie, that I eventually believed it myself. Unfortunately, that particular fabrication had unexpected and far-reaching consequences in my adult life.

I often wonder if my mother was capable of understanding that, in the wrong hands, imagination and creativity were tools that could also lead to self-destruction? But was this really her fault? Perhaps I just never figured out how to use the tools correctly? While my mother often used those castles in the sky to create magical stories that lifted spirits or gave comfort to dying children, I used them to deceive myself, an act which almost destroyed a life I had worked so hard to build.

Maybe it is wise to ask myself—in view of what I know about myself—should I really be so consumed by the existence of the secret and feel so wronged about something my mother never told me, when there are certainly things that I have lied about and kept secret?

A New Beginning

When I look back to the time I lived in Australia, it is hard to see any hints or clues of a secret. Months after my breakup with Janek, I began dating again and then met the true love of my life. He was smart, funny and cute and he was the first boyfriend my mother truly adored. He worked during the day and studied at Melbourne University at night. It did not take me long to realize that he was the one.

Soon after we started dating, I got a promotion and was put in charge of sorting out applications to Toorak Teachers' College. I was surprised to see that aside from the fact that they all passed English, most had Matriculation grades far worse than mine! I shared this with my boyfriend and wondered if I should also apply. A Teachers Certificate was not a law degree, but certainly better than no academic credentials at all. Could I somehow manage to get into a College?

"If you are seriously thinking of applying, the Minister of Education's office is next door, why don't you just go and explain your situation and see what happens!" he said.

I did just that. The next day, the Minister's secretary handed me an acceptance letter. I was to start college next week! My boyfriend and I laughed all the way home and I could not wait to share this great news with my parents. Dad was very excited, but Mom, looking very disappointed, asked "Really, Teachers College? A teacher? What kind of profession is that?"

Caught off guard, I had no response. Regardless, the next Monday I took the tram to Toorak and entered College. It was not long before I realized that I made the right choice. I loved kids and I found helping them learn very exciting. It gave me a sense of doing something worthwhile, and right away I knew that teaching was certainly the right profession for me. I successfully completed my first year, I was truly in love for the first time, my baby brother was delightful and my parents seemed happy. A new phase of my life had begun.

After graduating, I got a job in an elementary school in the outer suburbs. I was to teach second and third grade combined. I had twenty-nine children in my class and soon realized that while most of the third graders knew how to read, only a few of the second graders did. I devised a plan: The kids were divided into two groups and while I taught something new to one group, the older kids would read to the other group. In the afternoon all the children would participate in social studies, art and anything else that they could do together. It seemed to work and I was happy with the progress the children were making.

After four months, I was informed by the principal of the school to expect a routine visit from a supervisor. Only a few days later, that is exactly what happened. He slipped in a few minutes after class started, sat quietly through the day, and wrote furiously in his notebook. I was very nervous and even more so when, at the end of the day, I was summoned to the principal's office. The supervisor introduced himself and then offered some compliments on the discipline I kept and how well all the children dealt with math. And then said "Although I am very pleased with your methods, the enthusiasm that the children display when you assign a new task, the progress the children are making, and the fact that the second graders read so well, I find one thing a little troublesome"

I stiffened and held my breath. After coughing, sneezing and then blowing his nose, he proceeded "Many of the children in both grade two and three, now read with a Polish accent"

The principal looked at the inspector and I looked at him, ready to be fired on the spot. Instead, both started laughing so hard that I had to join in. After a short silence, I shared a story I heard my mother tell many times.

When Mom was three, her grandparents wanted her to learn German since all of her maternal family spoke it. They hired a tutor who was highly recommended by a friend. Mom was a fast learner, and she picked it up very quickly. However, soon after, she began to stammer. Several visits to various doctors did not solve the problem, and the family was at a loss as to what to do. They decided that perhaps the German tutor could help. The family gathered together on the day they arranged to meet with him and handed over all the suggestions from the many doctors they had consulted. The tutor read these very carefully and when asked for comments replied "I do-do-nnnn't thh-thh-thh-ink that I cc-cannn hh-help"

The principal, supervisor and I laughed for a long time. Not only did I keep my job but I also got a promotion—my assignment for the following year would be at a school in the suburb where I lived. Halfway through that school year I got engaged, and two months after that, my fiancée was offered a job in the US, beginning as soon as the company obtained a work permit for him. We married in December, 1968 (I was now teaching third grade in a school much closer to my home), and, just after that, we were informed that our move was all arranged and we would leave for the US in May, 1969.

For the second time in my life, I felt indescribable excitement as we arrived at the Commodore Hotel on 42nd St in New York City. My husband and I had read so much about the exciting New York but now we would see it all with our own eyes— Central Park, the Empire State Building, the Statue of Liberty, the Guggenheim, Carnegie Hall, and Fifth Av with the famous Tiffany's store. After sleeping just a few hours after our arrival in New York, we decided to go out, even though it was only six in the morning. It was Memorial Day weekend and the hotel was just by Grand Central Station. We were in the heart of that famous place!

But the sight that greeted us as we walked out of our hotel was horrifyingly disgusting! There were garbage cans and bags piled along the sidewalks of 42nd St. and even Fifth Avenue. Some piles were even taller than us! We walked along the avenue of my dreams, now covered in foul-smelling rubbish, and passed a grey building with empty display windows. I murmured to my husband "If that turns out to be Tiffany's, I'll cry"

It was. I did not cry, but I was terribly disappointed. When I spotted a policeman on the corner of Fifty-Seventh St., I ran over and, pointing to the trash that lined the street, I asked "Is it always like that? We just moved to New York from Australia and the city does not resemble anything we read about."

In a lovely Irish accent, the policeman replied "Don't you worry, miss, there is a garbage strike going on right now! Go home and come back in a day or so and you will see a different New York—I promise you'll love it."

He was absolutely right. I fell in love not just with New York, but with everything about the United States of America. The people were open and warm and the population was so diverse. While walking the streets of the city, we heard many different languages, saw people of color and people from Asian countries, as well as from all over Europe. No one marveled at my accent and anyone who asked where I was from, never used a disparaging tone. All were friendly and just curious. I loved being questioned about my background, since it inevitably led to some very interesting encounters. Though I had not been in America for a long time, I felt at home almost right away and wanted to meet as many Americans as possible.

After a couple of weeks of exploring New York City, we moved to Queens and my husband began his new job and, at some point a little later, we connected with my husband's childhood friends who came from Poland in the 1950s and some in 1968. They all lived in Brooklyn, so we decided to move there as well. But staying at home made me feel restless and I knew I needed to find a job so that I could feel as if I was contributing. When I overheard my Jewish neighbor tell her friend that the Jewish school her children attended was looking for a third-grade teacher, I called and made an appointment to be interviewed.

The principal, dressed in the Orthodox garb, flinched and quickly stepped back when I extended my hand to greet him. He would not look at me when he asked about my qualifications and background. As soon as I finished talking, he said, "In our school, we want the children to be educated not just in academic subjects, but also Jewish traditions, culture, etc. You told me that you taught third grade, said you are Jewish, and a child of Holocaust survivors, but you are not a Jew like any of us"

He said goodbye, turned around, and left without ever lifting up his head. I had no previous encounters with Jewish Orthodox people and did not know what to make of his behavior so I went to visit my Jewish neighbor and related what had transpired at the interview.

"You wanted to shake hands with an Orthodox rabbi!?" she exclaimed and I could not decide whether the look on her face was that of horror or disgust.

"Don't you know that the Orthodox Jews do not touch strangers, especially those of the opposite sex? I have never met anyone who didn't know that! No wonder he told you that you are not a Jew!"

That evening, at a gathering of our friends, all Jewish but not religious, I related that conversation, as well as the events of the interview. Though we all agreed that religion does not define our Jewish identity, none could articulate what did. At some point, however, one of my closest friends who prided himself on his Polishness as much as my mom did, spoke up, "The problem is that most of us don't really know what Jewish identity means. To the non-Jews, the mere fact that our ancestors were Jewish, makes us too Jewish to be one of them. To the observant Jews, our ancestry does not matter but the fact that we are not religious, makes us not Jewish enough. So, my fellow Polish Jews, we are screwed and it seems that we don't belong anywhere."

It took me years to see what he meant. Until I moved to the USA I never questioned what Jewish identity meant to me. Being the child of two Holocaust survivors, it should surely have meant something? My relative neutrality concerning my own Jewishness may have been an unintended, or perhaps intended, consequence of my mother's attitude towards her own heritage. She always seemed far more proud of her Polish heritage than her Jewish. Was her focus on her Polishness and her downplaying of any negative remarks directed at me and my family simply to limit my own experience of antisemitism? Or maybe there was something else that compelled her to ignore our Jewishness. Something perhaps that made her ashamed of it, or herself? Again, my imagination may be getting the better of me. The humiliations she, or any Jew, experienced during the Holocaust could have very easily resulted in conflicted feelings towards Jewishness, even if there was no secret complicating matters.

After I moved to New York, any uneasiness about my identity seemed to disappear. I was working and building a new life with my husband. I had taken off and was soaring along. In stark contrast, when I returned to Australia to visit my family, every time I looked in the mirror, all I saw was an amateur counterfeit of my mother, but one without a voice.

The Mother I No Longer Recognized

Sometime after we moved to New York, I decided to go back to college. Although I was happy with my Teaching Diploma and I loved teaching, I was now going to prove myself! I was going to get an American Bachelor's degree. After reviewing my transcripts, the admissions people at Brooklyn College suggested I had enough credits to enter a Master's program, but I really wanted an American Diploma in my hand so I insisted. It was a satisfying decision. I loved Brooklyn College and my life in NY.

I gave birth to our first child, a son, only a few hours after my very last exam and missed the graduation ceremony, so I had to go to the college to pick up my BS in Education diploma. As soon as I did, the first phone call I made was to Mom.

Upon hearing my exciting news all she said was "Once I had you, I was forced to forget all my ambitions."

I cannot remember how long and what we talked about after, but when I hung up, I cried. I could do no right and no matter what I did, she never gave me any credit. There was no use for self-pity, I told myself, yet something within me boiled over and the strongest desire to prove to her that I was as good as she was or maybe even better, took over.

But Mom had proven on many occasions that she had such a vast knowledge in so many subjects! She had read almost every book and heard of every poem I was assigned in high school. I still remember the shock I got the day I called Mom and mentioned that one of the courses I was taking in teacher's college required the reading of "Crime and Punishment."

"Do you know what the precursor to Dostoyevsky's "Crime and Punishment" was?" she asked.

I did not.

"On the 16th of November 1849, he had been sentenced to death for the crime of engaging in anti-government activities linked to a radical intellectual group. Just as the firing squad raised their guns, he was granted a reprieve,"

I was stunned, though I should not have been. Many times, especially when she was with friends, she would quote passages from books and recite poems she had learned as a child, and deliver them not just in Polish, but German as well. Her favorite poets were Goethe, Tuwim, and Mickiewicz. I think it was when I was in eighth grade, still in Poland, and came home very excited and told her that I had been given the honor to get up on stage and recite the "Kłotnia" portion of "Pan Tadeusz." She asked me to read the passage to her. I began without looking at the text and she joined in.

"Wojski, chlubnie skończywszy łowy, wraca z boru

A Telimena, w głębi samotnego dworu

Zaczyna polowanie. Wprawdzie nieruchoma

Siedzi z założonymi na piersiach rękoma"

Word for word, pausing slightly at each coma, her voice strong and softer where necessary, she recited the rest. I stopped reading and just listened to her, simply mesmerized. She remembered all this so many years later? How many people can do that? And she had so many other talents as well. She wrote satirical, amazingly witty poems about each of her friends. I heard Mom recite them on many occasions when I came to Australia, but had no idea how many there were, and how good they were until I began clearing out her house after she died. There were at least five notebooks filled with them! Usually written in honor of a friend who celebrated a birthday, or a couple who were celebrating their anniversary, all were hysterically funny, but never cruel. Those were the traits I always so admired and knew that I did not have. How is it possible that with all those talents Mom still felt that she had missed out? Was it because she never held an important job or that an academic degree meant so much to her?

On one of my many visits to Australia, my "aunts and uncles" (that is what I always called my parents' closest friends), came over to visit with us. All seemed very surprised that I now had a job and was no longer a stay-at-home Mom.

One of my "aunts" asked, "So did you go back to teaching?"

"No, I work as a court interpreter"

"A court Interpreter?" she asked, "What exactly does this involve?"

"I translate for Polish clients who don't know English or at least cannot fully understand what the charges are and what is being said to them when they appear in court"

"But doesn't this require knowledge of legal terminology? Exams?"

"Yes to both," I answered.

"We had no idea," my 'aunt' Erna said and, turning to Mom, asked "Why didn't you tell us, it sounds fascinating"

"Oh, it's a part-time job only, and it isn't half as interesting as you think. She is dealing mostly with drunks who then get a traffic ticket or something like that."

While my aunts kept asking me more questions, Mom left the room.

A couple of years later, when that same 'aunt' asked about my job, I told her that I had quit it so I could go back to college and was now taking courses toward a Master of Liberal Arts degree. She and all present there seemed as stunned as I was. Mom was again the first person I called after being accepted into the program. I was barraged with questions, and they were all very excited for me and wondered why Mom again had not shared this with them. Had this become a pattern, I asked myself? Once the guests left, I asked her about it. I do not recall what she said to me but it left me shaking. No, that is not exactly true—I was furious.

When my husband asked me why, I could not verbalize it. But I was inconsolable and had never felt so down and as angry at her as I did then. I kept thinking, "What mother would not celebrate her child's achievement? Why does she make everything I accomplish seem so insignificant?"

When I was already in my third year of a Ph.D. program, my mother called to tell us that she had been diagnosed with lung cancer and would have to undergo radiation therapy. She sounded very distraught and scared, and my husband and I agreed that we should go to Australia.

The chairman of my department was furious and would not hear of my request to interrupt my studies for a while. "You already had one interruption from the program when your youngest had to undergo treatment for Hodgkin's and now you are asking to take the whole semester off? I will not allow it." But my sense of duty and obligation was far stronger than the desire to get a Ph.D. and I told him that nothing would stop me from going to Australia to help my mother.

Mom had lost a lot of weight and, for the first time, did not seem to have the energy and stamina that I had seen all my life. Although I decided to stay this time with my husband's family, we spent a lot of time with Mom and hosted many dinners for family and sometimes friends. During one of those evenings when Mom's friends and our adopted family came for dinner, we were talking about Polish Literature and when I mentioned that I was planning on writing my Ph.D. dissertation on Czeslaw Milosz, the Polish Nobel Prize poet, the conversation at the table halted and someone asked "Ph.D.? Don't you first need a Master's!?" and someone else asked, "When did you decide to go back to University and how come we don't know anything about it?"

At that point, I looked at my husband and knew he was thinking what I was thinking, but all I said was "I'll tell you about it some other time, now it is time to enjoy our dinner."

What else was there to say? But, something stronger was stirring within me, emotions that were foreign and disturbing. I had never experienced anything like it before and, once Mom went to bed, I went back to the kitchen and probably had far too many glasses of wine. I slept through the night with no nightmares. We continued to visit every day and had dinner with her every evening. At some point, Mom asked me about some of my friends whom she had not seen for a long time and asked if we could invite them for dinner, I hesitantly agreed. Only on the condition that I would take care of the shopping, cooking and cleaning, so that she could enjoy it as a guest.

"But, they will be waiting for my gnocchi, you know how they always loved them," she said knowingly.

In response to her protests, I said "Mommy, it is a lot of work and you are just not fit for it now. Please relax, and let me do it all."

Protesting and mumbling something under her breath, she agreed and when she went to lie down and rest, my husband and I went shopping. That evening, when I had almost everything ready and the table was set, Mom walked in and asked what we were having for dinner.

"Butternut squash soup, manchego and apple salad, and garlic sauce pappardelle and broiled salmon"

"I bet no one will enjoy that!' she exclaimed and walked out.

Just before I was to serve the main course, Mom joyfully announced to my assembled friends "I have made your favorite gnocchis, so please enjoy your salad while I get them ready."

I was stunned and followed her to the kitchen "Mommy, why and when did you manage to make gnocchis?"

She looked at me with something of a triumphant expression on her face and replied "You will see, no one will eat your salmon once I serve the gnocchis"

When everyone was devouring them, as she had promised, she turned to me and loudly stated "I told you, no one will eat your food!"

I felt like someone just stabbed me.

I could not fall asleep that night and forced myself to think of my childhood, the magical mommy, of castles in the sky. But instead of sleeping, I had a sudden flashback. When I was five, I learned a poem by Tuwim, the renowned Polish poet. When Mom was finally satisfied with my diction, she decided that I would recite it at the next dinner party. Before she served the food, she hoisted me onto the coffee table and announced to her guests that they were in for a little treat.

Even though I was nervous, I bowed, just like she had taught me, and in a loud and confident voice announced "I will now recite "Lokomotywa" (In English, Locomotive) by Julian Tuwim."

I did well for a while, trying to annunciate the way Mom taught me, to pause when needed, and stress the parts that were repetitive. I tried very hard, as I did not want to disappoint her. But I was nervous and somewhere in the middle of the poem I forgot my lines. I looked to her for help. Without a word, she took me off the table, climbed up, finished reciting the poem, looked at me and said, "That is how it was supposed to be done."

I was sent to bed and Mom did not come to kiss me goodnight.

I had always thought that when I was younger my mother was magical and charming and there was nothing bad about her. But the more I began to think about my youth, and the different things that she had done, the more that image of her began to crack. I thought that I was so angry at her because she had changed so drastically. But I soon realized that my memories of her, both then and now, are so shrouded in dissonance that it becomes harder and harder to get a clear picture of her. Everything I remember about her seems to have become nothing more than distortions of my image of the past: the survivor, the magical storyteller, the unfaithful wife, the charming entertainer, the aloof aristocrat, the good Samaritan, and the mother with a secret never to be revealed; which or any of these were her true self? Was she all of them at once or none at all? Are all these nothing more than distractions from the real truth, where, perhaps, the secret might lie?

On the day my husband and I drove Mom for her first radiation treatment, we were delighted to see that, even under such circumstances, Mom happily engaged the nurse and the X-ray technician in conversation as soon as they came to get her. An hour or so later, as we were about to leave, the nurse remarked to me that as soon as she saw my mother, she guessed Mom must have been a model and was delighted when Mom confirmed it. I said nothing and smiled, but I could not believe that Mom made up something so outrageous. As we walked out, I asked her why she had lied about being a model. Looking quite shocked, she asked, "But you knew that I modeled fur coats, no?"

I could not recall any such time, so Mom reminded me "You know that I own a fur jacket, a very expensive one, right? Well, it did not cost me a penny—it was the payment for modeling this particular jacket. The furrier gave it to me after he sold so many, as all these women wanted one after they saw me model it. The owner even said to me later that I was the best model he ever had. You do remember that don't you? So stop asking me why I lied—I DID NOT LIE!"

When I gently pointed out that modeling a fur coat once, in a friend's house, was not exactly the same as having been a model, she got angry and retorted "But I did model, didn't I? And that evening they sold far more coats than ever before, mainly because every woman wanted to look like me!"

She smiled somewhat condescendingly, shrugged her shoulders and dismissively waved her still beautiful hand in a way that left no doubt she was right. I left it at that—it did not matter after all, except that I began to recall how frequent such creative narratives had been in the past few years and that when she somehow involved me in them, how angry I became.

I remember calling my mother to tell her about a funny incident when my husband and I went to dinner at a well-known restaurant in NY. The entry hall was pretty crowded and just after we had our coats checked, a tall gentleman handed his to my husband, obviously mistaking him for the coat valet. Quickly realizing he made a mistake, he smiled shyly, took the coat back, and handed it to the wardrobe valet. The man was Alan Alda!

A few months later, on another visit to Australia, once again during a gathering of friends at my parents' home, Mom began to tell that particular story. She first described the fancy restaurant but greatly exaggerated the lavish decor which included paintings by famous artists on the walls, much fancier china, more intricate flower arrangements on the tables, etc. In that much more elaborate and exciting version, she was there with us. She accurately related my husband's encounter with the famous actor, but then her creative imagination kicked in and Alan Alda, realizing his mistake, apologized profusely, introduced himself and, after shaking my hand, invited all of us to have dinner with him.

"And that is why," she added, "My daughter now can get a reservation at this restaurant any time, while an ordinary person has to wait for months."

I did not want to embarrass her in front of her friends so I did not bother to correct her, or point out that she had perhaps mixed up some of the facts with the time a close friend of my husband came to visit us in Chicago.

We knew that food was his passion, that he owned a couple of small restaurants and food stands in Stockholm and that at one time he even catered to the king of

Sweden, so way ahead of his visit, I managed to get a reservation at a restaurant that was considered to be the best in Chicago at the time. He loved the ambiance and the French cuisine and just as he mentioned how much he would enjoy seeing the kitchen and meeting the chef, the restaurant owner's wife appeared at our table, asking if we were happy with our meal. We expressed our delight and I, without a moment's hesitation, introduced our friend as a restaurateur in Sweden and casually mentioned that he even catered to the King of Sweden and quickly added that he was really interested in seeing the kitchen and would love to meet the chef.

Madame Banchet was extremely gracious and took us all there. This was a delightful end to a superb evening since our friend's wish had been granted, and from then on I could get a reservation any time, not only for us but also for our friends. I soon became the go-to person whenever any of them could not get a table at La Francaise. And that was the only part of my mom's version that was accurate.

As Mom's disease progressed, she felt more and more entitled to do and say anything at all. When I would object, her response was always "My doctor told me that at my age I should have no restraints and do and say as I please"

So, she continually invented new stories and although these were more entertaining than the facts, when she involved me, I felt embarrassed and got angry with her all over again.

"I am sorry. I really do that just to make everything sound more fun. I understand your frustration but please do not be angry with me," she cried and apologized profusely when I told her how I feel. But a few days later there would be another creative narrative.

It continued every time I came to visit and I would continue to get very angry, then feel terribly guilty about it—she was a sick woman! I kept asking myself why I was so mad at Mom all the time? She had been like this all her life and I had either never noticed or minded, so why now? Why couldn't I control my temper? But no matter how hard I tried I could not come up with an explanation. I just know that every time I came to Australia to visit her, I felt distraught and confused and, after a while, simply put, devastated.

Another time, while we were sitting with our friends and talking about art, I shared with them how our recent purchase of some old paintings turned out to be very exciting.

"My husband's cousin had a friend who worked as a curator in a museum in NY and one day she called to ask if we were interested in buying some paintings. The museum was offering some art for sale to their employees and her friend bought several and was willing to sell us a couple. We bought three, but only two of them looked good in our house, so we stored the third.

A few years later when we moved to a bigger house, we took that painting out of the basement. The colors of the flowers were perfect for our dining room, but it must have been too damp there and the painting was slightly warped, so we took it to an art restorer. Several weeks later, we got a call from him. After the usual polite greeting, he said "Are you sitting down, if not, please do"

I was sure he was going to tell me that he ruined the painting, but, instead, he said, "When we started working on it, the flowers started peeling off and we realized that they were painted over something underneath. When we carefully removed them we saw that we were right. We examined it carefully and we think it might be an old painting by Whistler. We are not sure and would have to call on an expert, but it is beautiful. If you decide you would like to do this, we could bring him to your house."

We picked up the painting—a handsome young merchant dressed in an elegant fur-trimmed cloak and at the top, on the right side, a small landscape. Maybe it was Whistler? It somehow did not seem possible that the museum would have missed that! A couple of years later, we had a dinner party and one of our guests was an art professor. He was sitting right across the painting, and at some point asked about the painting and when I told the story, he got up to examine it. He was certain it was not a Whistler."

All of my friends found this amusing and one asked, "But why wouldn't you ask a real expert?"

"I think it is a far better story if that answer remains a mystery, don't you think?" I answered.

Before anyone had a chance to comment, my mom said, "You see, my daughter turned out just like me. I bet she made this up after she heard me tell my friends about a painting that our neighbor bought at the seaside in Poland!"

I was so taken aback, humiliated, shocked and then outraged, but before I had a chance to protest, she told her story about Julian's Painting.

For a long time after that incident, I kept recalling the many times Mom has derided me in front of others and how, whenever I confronted her, she always apologized and assured me that she never meant to hurt me. But her behavior did not change and I would again feel angry and tell myself that I hate her. I often wondered about those feelings later, because deep down I always knew I could never stop loving her. Maybe if you truly love a person you can forgive them for anything? But, can you forget?

Could that also be the way that Dad felt about his wife after she left us with Julian? Their relationship is almost as much of a mystery as the secret itself. I cannot help thinking back to the day that Daddy, even though his colon cancer was already so advanced that he was bedridden, tried to console me after some interaction with my mother had left me distraught. It was getting dark but Dad asked to please not turn on the light. As I snuggled up to him, he slowly relaxed and I realized that the darkness allowed him to talk to me without having to face me. In a whisper, he began "Every night now I see him in my sleep and feel so guilty. And then other memories just keep coming—Dziubuś (*his favorite name for me, which loosely translates to little beak*), there are so many things I regret. Memories can be so cruel. They keep haunting me and punishing me. I have to confess that I always envied your Mother's gift to remake them into something not just acceptable, but beautiful. Do you understand?

He took my hands in his and was silent for a while but then he told me he had a confession to make.

"Dziubuś, we have always been open with each other and now I need to share something with you that has been bothering me all these years. I couldn't bring myself to talk about it before, but maybe now you should hear this. It might make you hate me, but there is a chance it will make you feel less guilty about all those fights you are having with your Mom."

He seemed deep in thought and upset and I kept telling him not to worry, that nothing he tells me will ever bother me. He thought for a while, hesitated, but began "My little brother and I were on our way to a hiding place where my parents felt the Nazis could not find us. I had a loaf of bread in each pocket, when I saw a group of Jews lying on the ground, surrounded by German guards. They were all old, very dirty and obviously starving. They were begging for food. Among them was my beloved uncle, and he was praying out loud and begging God for even just one bite of bread! But I just stood there! How could I have been so heartless?"

My heart almost broke, but all I could do was hug and kiss him and keep repeating "Daddy, you did the right thing. Otherwise, I would not have had you."

I could not see what this had to do with my relationship with my mother, so I continued talking to him "Daddy, you must remember that if you even tried to get the bread to him, you would have been shot right there! I know you and am sure you would have risked your life, but your eleven-year-old brother was just behind you and he, too, would have been killed so you did what you should have done. Think about it, wasn't it right to think of your little brother first? Please, stop feeling guilty"

"That is funny, because this is why I told you this story and exactly what I wanted you to understand."

He seemed lost in thoughts, but then asked me to sit close to him, put his arms around me and said "I don't know if it is a good decision on my part, but I want to tell you something else. Something that I have been thinking about telling you for a while, but every time I tried, I changed my mind. Even today, I told you about my uncle because I did not have the heart to share this with you. But now I will, even if it's not the right decision. When you were about six or seven months old, your mother ran away from us with another man. It took me a few days to find a woman who was nursing her own baby and who was willing to take you in while I went to look for your mother. I had no clue where she was so it took me a while, but I found her and brought her home to us."

I think that at that point I must have gone into shock, because I cannot remember if he said anything else or if I asked any questions. So, I don't know with whom, where, or how long Mom was away. But, I do know that her trip with Julian was not the only time that my mother had abandoned us. I am not sure why he thought this information might benefit me. And he certainly could not have suspected how much more material for speculation his revelation would provide later in my life. If only I had the foresight to ask him more questions, but I never asked about it again. Why? Because I saw how hard it had been for him to talk about it? Because I was terrified and tried to protect myself? What if that had been just another tiny scratch on the surface of the secret? What else was hidden underneath?

That night, in my dream, I heard something that began as murmuring but soon turned into an almost hypnotic chorus of the most beautiful voices repeating the refrain "You were not wanted!" Why would she abandon me when I was so young, and once again later in life? Was the secret that I was not my mother's child? I thought about that for a long time and, eventually, it drew out another incident from my childhood that had happened after the raid on our house, following my father's arrest. The morning after the raid, when I was helping my mother clean up the bedroom, I came across a birth certificate that had my given names, my birth date, the last name was not Bild, but Sakowski. Puzzled, I questioned my mother. Without hesitation, she replied "To be safe during the war, your daddy took on a Polish name, now hurry and let's clean up the mess."

I was satisfied and never thought about it, but now I wonder. Bild is a German surname, so why change it? Is it possible that one, or both of my parents are not actually my parents at all? My brother had laughed at me when I wanted to have his DNA tested, saying that no matter what it proved it would change nothing about our relationship and life. If I was not my parents' biological child, would that change anything? What if that mother I no longer recognized had never really been my mother at all?

Another Castle in the Sky

My husband and I came to Australia when my older niece was to become a Bat Mitzvah. Mom was very sick and did not have much time left. As we had done for the past two years, we stayed with my husband's sister and brother-in-law, but took Mom for her chemo treatments and all other appointments, did the grocery shopping, cooked and ate every meal together, but we left her after dinner.

Two days after Bat Mitzvah, as I had done every day since we arrived, I called to see if she wanted us to pick up something for lunch or if she preferred to go out. But the phone was busy and for the next forty-five minutes, it seemed that Mom was still talking. How typical of her, I thought, and made the decision we would all just have lunch out. I called again around 11:00 AM to give Mom time to get ready. The phone was still busy. When I dialed fifteen minutes later and once again heard the busy signal, I got nervous and decided we should go over to check on her.

I rang the doorbell three times and when she did not open it, I dug out the key that was always under the mat. But the screen door was locked and I could not get to the front door. I tried the gate to the backyard, but that was also locked. I was getting frustrated and then I got really worried. Shaking, I screamed at my husband "Something is wrong! Call my brother!"

Rob lived just a few blocks away and when he came over he laughed "Mom is probably in the shower" he said, "What's wrong with you? I never knew you to panic so easily"

I just wanted him to hurry up and open the door.

The house was peaceful and quiet when we entered. None of the usual aromas of cooking, no sound of classical music playing somewhere in the background. The bathroom was empty and, like the rest of the house, spotlessly clean and neat. Not even a hairdryer or makeup on the counter. It seemed like the house had not been used at all. I ran into the bedroom—empty. I then remembered that, since Dad died, Mom had been sleeping on the pull-out couch in the guest bedroom. It was facing the backyard and she said she felt safer there.

I let out a sigh of relief when I saw how peacefully asleep she was. Why did I not notice how pale and skinny and fragile she had gotten? Looking at her the guilt I felt was unbearable. I leaned over and tried to wake her, but she did not respond. At that point, my husband walked in. "Anita, stop, she is dead"

I refused to hear him and tried waking her one more time, but my brother pulled me away. When the ambulance arrived and the crew casually lifted Mom off her bed I became hysterical.

"She is so tiny, she'll break" I kept screaming as I followed them to the door. "This my mother you are handling, be more respectful!"

I kept repeating this even after they drove away. I was back in the back bedroom when I noticed the almost empty vial of sleeping pills on her nightstand. I pointed this out to my husband and my brother and they both dismissed my concerns. But I could not stop wondering. Had my mother decided to meet death on her own terms, before the pain took over? Was this something she planned for a while? Or, and the thought twisted my stomach, did she do it because she felt abandoned by me?

For most of my childhood and even young adulthood, I worshipped the ground she walked on. All I saw was an enigmatic creature, mysterious and magical and I wanted to be just like her, tried hard to emulate her, and more importantly, craved her approval. Yet, that approval was always distant and unattainable, so in a way, my pursuit of her acceptance had been my own castle in the sky. An ephemeral vision I dreamed of and wished for with all my heart and I constantly tried to convince myself I would have it one day, just as my mother had taught me. None of this changed for a very long time but, at some point, a different portrait of that person was revealed, one that had been long hidden underneath the surface, just like Julian's painting and the one hanging in our own dining room. An image of a complex, bitter and insecure person, afraid of her past.

I still loved her with all my heart, but our relationship changed drastically when I finally understood that while it is okay to build castles in the sky, these are not always attainable and might not be meant to be reached. As my mind lingers on that empty vial, I cannot help wondering what she was pursuing throughout her life? Did she ever find it before she found peace?

Not too long after my father died, Mom already had an admirer. He was ten years older and rather unappealing, but he made my mom happy. They were partners at bridge games, had a subscription to the opera and theater, and saw every new movie as soon as it appeared in the local theater. He once said to me "Do you know what the biggest advantage of being hard of hearing is?" When I said no, he cunningly smiled, "The ability to turn off a hearing aid whenever you want, do you know how easy this makes it to worship your Mother?"

I liked him a lot except when he sat in my Dad's chair in the kitchen.

Family Reunion

Five years after my mother's death, and deep into my search, it still felt like I was no closer to the secret, even though I kept remembering more and more things from my past. It seemed that all I had was a fragmented view. It was like a puzzle where I had only found the most obvious pieces, but those that would reveal the hidden image remained lost to me. It seemed that everything I remembered only led to more questions. It did not help that my mother did not have any family or living friends who could help me uncover more answers and piece together the rest of the puzzle, that there was no one alive who could verify anything about my mother. At least that was what I thought until I attended the wedding of a friend's son and everything changed.

My husband and I flew to Boston where the wedding was taking place. It was a beautiful outdoor ceremony, as was the dinner that followed, and we were having a great time talking to the other guests seated at our table. We had known all of them for a long time and liked them, but only saw each other at functions organized by other friends, and our conversations were never of a personal nature. That evening, however, the discussion somehow turned to our parents. Upon hearing my mother's maiden name and the town she came from, Joseph, a man I had known for many years, mentioned he had a friend in Paris, Karol, with the same surname and that Karol's family also came from the same town as my mother.

At the mention of Karol's father's name and the title of the book his father wrote, I got very excited "I have that book on my bookshelf! A long time ago, my mom gave it to me as she had two copies. On the first page of mine, there is a handwritten note by a translator"

I quoted "Dear Zosia, your cousin Alek, recently passed away, so I am sending you his book as I know he wanted you to have it"

I told Joseph I had just presumed that the author was just another "cousin," but maybe not? Joseph scribbled down a phone number and explained that Karol was visiting a friend in the United States and that I should phone him.

"Alek told the translator that your Mother is his cousin, so maybe?"

It sounded good and I eagerly followed his advice. Although I was shaking with excitement at the prospect of finding a real cousin on my mother's side, I decided to proceed cautiously. A few years previously I had a rather unpleasant experience when I made a similar call:

While looking through a phone book for the number of a restaurant in NY, I suddenly came across a person with my maiden name. It is not a common name and, without thinking, I dialed the number. "Please forgive me," I said as soon as a man picked up the phone, "I have the same last name as you and thought we might be related"

"Interesting," he replied, "please go on."

I told him where my father's family came from.

"My family also came from the same region of Poland, but they left Poland in the 1920s," he said "but I still have many relatives living in Poland—do you"?

"No," I answered, "unfortunately, none of my family survived."

"All are dead? You have no family at all?"

"No one except my parents and my brother. Every member on my mother's and my father's side perished in the Holocaust," at that point, I quickly asked "My family is Jewish, are you?"

"Certainly not!!" and the phone went dead.

Though I knew that Karol was Jewish, when I phoned him the next day I still began cautiously "I have a book written by your father and there is a handwritten note on the first page..." and then I explained the whole situation

I was relieved when he responded amicably "I don't know anything about your Mother, but it definitely sounds like we are related. Maybe you should contact my cousins? In Israel and in Poland? I think it merits further investigation."

He gave me a couple of phone numbers and email addresses. After all those years of thinking that my mother's entire family had perished, I was really excited at the prospect of finally making contact with people who were real relatives. And, maybe, it was also a chance of finding something that might lead to more clues about the secret. But none of the people I contacted had ever heard of my mother.

I decided to search more carefully through my mother's various letters and photos I had brought home after she passed away. When I came across a picture of a big family that had been signed by each member, I was astounded when I realized that their last name was the same as my mother's maiden name! It had been taken in Israel in about 1974. I was even more shocked when I saw that the first names of the younger ones matched all of Karol's cousins that I had recently contacted. I sent a copy to each of them. None could shed any new light on how my mother got the photos. However, after hearing the little note from the translator of Karol's father's book, they all agreed that we must be related somehow. But how?

Karol suggested I get in touch with his cousin Hania who still lived in Poland. Since my husband and I had plans to visit Poland that month, I wrote to her and we agreed to meet for dinner. She, too, seemed puzzled and said she could not help me, but, as we were exchanging some basic information about our mothers, I had a sudden flashback of a sun-filled room and a young man sitting at the piano, playing one of my favorite Chopin ballads. He was so handsome that I, at the age of ten, fell madly in love.

"Do you have a brother whose name is Victor?" I asked Hania.

"Yes"

"And does he play the piano?

"Yes"

We were getting somewhere, I thought! But Hania quickly added that she had absolutely no recollection of that visit. Another dead end. But we decided to stay in touch.

A few months later, I got an invitation from Karol to join a family reunion that was to be held in Warsaw the following year. Most of the cousins were going to be there, he said, and perhaps we could solve how we are related. I accepted immediately.

I brought the book written by Karol's father, and the photo of the Israeli family, as well as photos of the paintings that were hanging in my parents' home and signed by Bella Szurek. I knew that this woman visited my mother in Australia and my mother even organized an exhibition of her paintings. I liked her work a lot, and her paintings, which had hung in my parents' house, were now in my living room.

I showed the photos of these to one of the cousins, Danny, who was Bella's son, but even he could not shed any new light on our connection. Sensing my frustration, another cousin, Nir, came to the rescue. Using the internet and consulting the Jewish Genealogy site, he found out that our great grandfathers were brothers! So I was very excited when I was told that all the cousins would meet that afternoon, bring photos and documents, and share stories about their families.

During the presentation, I listened in awe. It was amazing how much they knew about their parents, grandparents and even great grandparents, and how many photos they all had. But, it was not so surprising—no member of that family perished in the Holocaust or had been in a concentration camp. As the presentation progressed, I became more and more confused—the similarities between what my cousins were relating about their great grandparents and what I heard from Mom about her grandparents were far too strong. They even had the same first names? How could that be? Was it possible that Mother mixed up the families when she talked to me about her own grandparents?

But unlike my father, my mother always had such a good memory! About ten years before she died, someone at a party asked whether anyone knew who wrote the Polish poem, Snuc Milosc (in English, Spin Love). Mom not only answered immediately that it was Adam Mickiewicz but began reciting it!

Snuc Milosc Adam Mickiewicz	Spin Love (Translation by Clare Cavanagh)
Snuć miłość jak jedwabnik nić wnętrzem snuje, Lac ja z serca, jak źródło wodę z wnętrza leje, Rozwijać jak złota blache, gdy się kuje A ziarna zlorego, puszczac ja w glab, jak nurtuje	Spin love just as a worm spins silk from inside, And pour it from your heart as springs from bedrock flow. And spread it, frail as sheets of gold, hammered out wide

Zrodlo pod ziemia – w gore wiac nia, jak wiatr wieje,
Po ziemi ją rozsypać, jak się zboże sieje,
Ludziom piastować, jak matka swych piastuje'
Stąd bedzie naprzód moc twa, jak moc przyrodzenia,
A potem będzie moc twa, jak moc krzewienia.
Potem jak ludzi, jak moc aniołów.
A w końcu będzie jak moc Stwórcy stworzenia

From glittering seeds: and let it stream below and ride
With rivers underground, and blow high as winds blow:
And scatter like grains, which take deep roots and grow:
Nurse it for mankind as a does her child
And herewith grows your might – at first, like that of nature,
Than might exceeding all the elements: then vast
As power born of ceaseless generation:
Than might of humankind: of angels: and, at last
Might rivaling the Lord of All creation

Even at her advanced age, she did not miss a line. How could someone with such a fantastic memory mix up the names of her grandparents, uncles, or aunts? When I thought about it carefully, I realized that, for a long time, even before Fela revealed the existence of the secret, I suspected that some of what she shared with me about her family might have been embellished, exaggerated, or made up, though I am not sure when I began to have such doubts or why. Had I always suspected something subconsciously, or maybe it began while our relationship was slowly breaking down?

There is only one story, embellished or not, that is definitely true. And that is the heartbreaking account of Mom in Auschwitz. This had been confirmed by her friend Bronka, with whom she escaped. But what about everything else? After the reunion, I kept recalling every bit of what little she shared about her childhood and I became even more suspicious.

Mom never missed a chance to mention her background: Her maternal grandparents came from "aristocracy," they were very very rich, and were one of the most prominent families in Kalisz. Yet she never told me their last names, did not explain who their ancestors were, nor if they had any siblings or other relatives, or what exactly they did for a living. Some of what she had told me, now began to sound more like a movie script than events that could have happened to an ordinary person! How she had volunteered at the hospital at such a young age, how the head of the hospital personally taught her so much about medicine in such a short time, and her acceptance to a medical school in Berlin that she would have attended if the war had not started. Was any of that plausible, or just wishful thinking? Her castle in the sky?

Even when I got much older and began to have some doubts, I forced myself to believe it all. It was not until I discovered that there was a secret that I began to seriously question anything she had ever told me. True, she often told stories that were fabrications, but I had always thought that there was a clear distinction between those fabrications and her life. But now I wondered—was the ideal childhood she described to me, her own castle in the sky? Had she always been inclined to do that? Or, did she start building it once she realized that every one of her dreams was shattered?

I have never found any evidence that might confirm any of those doubts. But I cannot help wondering why my cousins, who were so interested in family history, and seemed to know every bit about it going back to the 1800s, had no idea about my mother's existence, though their parents obviously did? I could not think of a reasonable explanation, except that maybe when my mother had met their parents and told them her story, they did not believe her, for some reason? And that was why they did not bother mentioning her to their children? But Alek wanted her to have his book, and Bella did come to visit her when she came to Australia—something was definitely amiss.

The more I thought about it, the more I seriously began to consider the possibility that she had created a brand new past for herself, one that she always wished for. But it is also very probable that the childhood she described to me, did contain fragments of her previous life pieced together with chunks from other relatives' lives. The question was, "Why?" I thought back to how often Mother had insisted that imagination was far more important than facts, that being able to imagine and create was the most precious gift one could possess. Had she used this gift to create a more ideal family? To help her deal with...what? With the horrors of Auschwitz?

Or, did she invent all this after the war, in some twisted way to compensate for the unfulfilled ambitions that were so brutally squashed? Was the "before the war"

Zosia just a conscious creative process that my talented mother continuously worked and improved on? Like a storybook? Was that the SECRET? Or, perhaps, all of it had been the work of the subconscious? Because the truth was so unbearable she had to blank it out, and as time went on she became so invested in the process of creating a new life that she could no longer distinguish between truth and fiction? That could explain why she did not tell me about the family members who survived.

However, I might have just forgotten that Mom did show me these photos, presuming that those cousins in the pictures were just "cousins"? But if I had forgotten, she must have mentioned it so casually that I was convinced this was the case. Why? She knew how I always craved real family! I was already married and have been to Israel at least twice since 1974 and I know that I would have contacted them.

On the other hand, how is it that none of them remember her visit and don't even know of her existence? Danni, the son of the painter Bella who visited my mom in Australia, had never heard of her, even though my mother organized an exhibit of Bella's paintings! I know she bought some and many of my mother's friends bought some—I have at least four! In the book that Karol's father wrote there is a specific mention of my mother being a cousin, and yet Karol knows nothing about her?

Why did Mom tell me that both her parents were with her in the Łódź ghetto and were deported to Auschwitz together, when I found out that my grandfather had died in 1941 and was buried in the Łódź cemetery? When the reunion group decided to visit the cemetery I checked for myself as soon as I got there. The person in charge of the records confirmed that he had indeed been buried there in 1941. How could Mom have forgotten that? Is it possible the SECRET had something to do with that?

I was very shaken by all these questions and shared them with my newfound cousin's wife, Monique, on the last day of the reunion. I confessed how haunted I was by the many unanswered questions, especially the secret, and about what else I might not know. How do I explain to our three older grandchildren that whatever I had told them about my grandparents' Holocaust experience could be all a lie? What will I now tell my younger six grandchildren when they ask similar questions? And how can I write a memoir to help my children and grandchildren learn about their ancestors, if I can't be sure anything I know is true?

She listened very carefully and gently asked "Does knowing that your Mother made up things change anything about your memories, or your own experience? Do you really need to know everything that happened to her? Do you want to? How would any of what you find out change what you experienced? Press the delete button on the unknown, tell them what you were told and then write your story—a story of a child of two Holocaust survivors"

Her rational words helped me reconcile some of my doubts about writing this book, but did little to prevent the haunting feeling that occupied my mind when I thought about all that I did not know and the abiding mystery of the secret. In light of everything new I had learned, I began to review what I had already written and suddenly had another recollection from my childhood.

Once, when I threw a temper tantrum when Mom ignored one of many pleas to tell me a story about her family, she shared what she told me was a secret. Her father, Juda, was a socialist, and all of his family were as well. Her maternal grandparents considered this left-leaning family so beneath them that they severed all contact with their daughter when she insisted on marrying Juda, even though he was an educated Jew, an engineer. It was only when Mom was born and they fell in love with her right away, that they resumed the relationship and always made sure that Mom lived like a princess and lacked nothing at all. At some point later, when she repeated that story, she added that her father was sent to France by the engineering company he worked for and was away for ten years. Her sister Dorota was born when he finally came back and that is why there was such a big gap in age between her and her sister.

At that time, I had no reason to question any of it, but after everything I had learned, I could not help but wonder. It seems unusual that he would leave his family for so long. Did he leave his wife and child? And is that why he was not with them in the Łódź Ghetto? Was Dorota not his child? Which part of this story was just another one of Mom's narratives? Why would she make up something like this?

Since I now suspected that anything slightly unusual about my mom's stories could have something to do with the secret, I decided to try and more carefully verify some of the details. In the Łódź Ghetto archives, I found some new information that confirmed that Dorota was indeed 10 years younger. But as I examined the records under the name Szurek more carefully, other details came to light that led to even more questions:

Szurek Zosia—birth, 17/03/1922, Hirten 20, (AUSG) 10/1/43

Szurek Brana—birth, /1894, Hirten 20, (GEST) 10/1/ 43

Szurek Dorota—birth, 29/10/1932, Hirten 20, (AUSG) 10/1/43

There was no record of my grandfather, Juda Szurek. But my mom had always said that both her parents were deported to Auschwitz, and that her sister, Dorota, was killed by the Germans when they found her during a raid. Confused, I looked even more carefully and found an entry in the archives that truly shocked me:

Szurek Rosia—birth, 17/03/1922, Hirten 20, (ABG) 4/1/43

I had never heard of any Rosia. Who could this woman be, with the exact same birth date as my mother? At first glance, I thought that this must have been just a misspelling of Zosia or a mistake in the archive. But, when I double and triple-checked the meaning of the original German abbreviations, I saw that while my mother had been deported (AUSG) on October 1, 1943, her mother died (GEST) (or maybe was killed?) on October 1, 1943—the same day Mom was deported? And, Dorota, the sister my mother claimed was killed before the ghetto, seemed to have been deported along with her. Why would she invent a story describing the horrific death of her sibling?

But even more curious was the mysterious Rosia, who had been moved (ABG) to a new address on April 1, 1943, five months before the rest of the family? Is it possible that Mom had a twin sister? If she really existed, why did she move away from her mother and sister, and what happened to her after that? Did she get married? Was that the secret? Is it possible that Mom did not want to remember any of that? Especially that she had a twin? What happened to her? Did she survive? If she got married, was the name of her husband Sakowski—the name I saw on my birth certificate long ago? Maybe she had a child? And the child survived, but she did not? Am I that child?

If that was indeed true, it certainly could be the key to solving the mystery of the secret! And it would be almost a relief compared to some of the fantastical—and horrific—theories I have concocted. Is it possible this was why whenever I asked my mother to tell me the only story I really wanted to know, the one about her childhood, she immediately thought of something to distract me? And that is why she made up a tale about her idyllic childhood? But ended with "WWII put an end to all my dreams, that is all you need to know."

I can't help recalling now what she said to me shortly after I failed my matriculation exam and we talked about my choices, "You know that even as a child I wanted to be a doctor and always looked forward to the day I would be going to university. But when the nightmare of the war ended, I got married and had a child before I knew it. I was forced to forget that dream and all the others I might have had. Instead, I had to become a different person. I did and I managed, and so will you"

She seemed devastated. I remember vividly how she put both of her hands over her temples as if she suddenly got a horrible headache, and ran out. But what if I had misunderstood what caused her that pain? What if at that moment she remembered her twin sister? I can only imagine what horror Mom might have gone through. Had these horrific shadows from her past threatened her always, and had prevented her from being comfortable with her true self, so that she was forced to reinvent herself?

Jerzy Kosinski in his book, *Passion Play,* described memory as a "fraudulent bookkeeper"—one that "edits and shapes the experiences of the past into scenarios of its own." Could this apply to my mother? The question is—even if I could ever find out, do I really want to?

When Monique asked me if finding my mom's secret would change anything in my life, I told her that I didn't think so. But then, as had happened in my childhood, I began to have anxiety attacks. Despite my best attempts, I could not prevent my vivid imagination from inventing scenes of horrors that could turn my magical Mother into a monster. Of course, I did not want this to be true, and deep down did not believe it would be, but all I could think of was the movie *'Remember',* and convinced all my friends to see it.

'Remember' is a revenge drama that follows a 90-year-old Holocaust survivor, Zev Guttman. He lives in a nursing home, struggles with advancing dementia and grief over the recent loss of his wife, Ruth. Soon after her death, he gets a mysterious package containing a stack of money and a letter from his friend, Max, a co-resident in the nursing home who is also a Holocaust survivor. The letter describes a plan to find the sadistic guard who was responsible for the death of Zev's and Max's family. The monster now apparently lives under an assumed name, somewhere in the US. Max found three people with that name, but since he is incapable of leaving his home it is up to Zev to find those three and determine which one is the guard. Zev embarks on a cross-country hunt for the man responsible for the deaths of their families. His flaring episodes of dementia complicate the task and you hold your breath when he finds the first, then the second person with that name. But nothing prepares you for the shock that follows the encounter with the third man. "I recognize your voice," Zev tells the Nazi, but instead of looking frightened, the Nazi smiles, embraces him, and tells him that he knew they would meet again and recognize each other despite their new looks and assumed identities. It takes a few seconds, but then you gasp in horror. It is Zev who is THE monster!

How could anyone be so perfidious, and be able to get away with it? Take on a Jewish identity and live his life as a Jew? Marry one and raise a Jewish Family? How will his children ever be able to deal with the fact that their father was not just a fraud but a MONSTER? Even if the father they knew was a good and decent man, can they ever forget he was responsible for the deaths of so many? And could they then ignore the insidious motives for his new identity? Could they make themselves believe that a person can change so drastically? Or that he had done this to atone for the sins he committed?

I am so grateful to our son Ben, who convinced me to take the DNA test. I know that I am almost one hundred percent Jewish, so my mother and father must have been too. I also know that my father stood by his wife all his life, no matter what, and I am convinced that he knew a lot more about what happened to her than he ever let on.

Bar Mitzvah

Despite everything, it was hard not to notice the antagonism between my parents, and it became even starker toward the end of my father's life. Never did I wonder more how they managed to stay together so long, than in the time that followed my father's diagnosis with colon cancer. I came to Australia to be there when Dad met with the oncologist. I was devastated when he told us there was not much hope, but when Dad turned to me and, with a mischievous smile said, "Dziubuś, please remember, Hitler could not finish me and neither will cancer. I've dealt with far worse, so please, chin up!"

I believed him. He did last far longer than anyone predicted. But after four years he got gradually worse and when the doctors did not think he would last a year, my husband and I decided to once again go to Australia, this time for a month, to spend some quality time with him. He was very weak and skeletally thin, but as was the norm for him, when asked how he was doing, he always "felt great" and he seemed to get better after each visit from his friends and mine. Seeing how his spirits improved when he had visitors, I thought it might be good to move Dad's bed to the living room and suggested it to Mom.

She was aghast "You expect me to mess up the living room with a bed? Where should I entertain my friends when they come to visit?"

I was a little taken aback by what I thought was a ridiculous question in the circumstances "What's wrong with the kitchen?" I asked. 'Isn't that where you all usually sit?"

"Only when we eat and drink," Mom replied angrily "but after, we always sit in the living room."

"But don't you think Dad would also like to be with everyone in the living room?" I asked.

"Do you think anyone will be able to enjoy looking at a dying man?" she was getting very angry.

"Mommy, just think" I said, trying not to lose my temper, "Those people are coming to see Daddy as well"

"That's what you think." was her reply as she walked away.

I decided to ignore her and asked Dad what he thought of the idea of being moved to the living room. I still smile when I remember the look of sheer happiness on his face. And, so, despite my mother's objections, my husband and I moved Dad and all his medications to the living room. The next day, when some of my parents' friends came to visit, Mom tried to usher them to the kitchen as soon as they walked in. But the living room was just off the front foyer and they all saw that Dad was now in the living room, all immediately asked to sit there. For a few days, Mom tried again to get visitors to come to the kitchen, only to hear that they came to visit Dad.

Mom was now very unhappy with me and whenever I tried to explain how much happier Dad seemed to be, her reply was "I know he is your favorite and you care only for his happiness and not mine."

And, to myself, I thought "Yes, you are right."

How could she have been so petty to begrudge a dying man the comfort of his friends? What happened to the woman I had worshipped? The woman who would take the shirt off her back to help a stranger in need? Did my father see how much she changed? Was there anything left of the woman that he had married? What was it that kept them together all those years despite everything?

Since I began to look for clues to solve the secret, I have thought a lot about both of my parents and I am sure that whatever my mother's secret is, it does not involve any atrocity against our people. My Dad would never have married her if he had even the slightest suspicion that this might have been the case

Although he rarely talked about the past, as he got older, and especially once I became a Mother, Dad often spoke of the importance of Jewish heritage and culture. His respect for these was most evident when it came to traditions, especially Bar and Bat Mitzvahs and nothing could have stopped him from attending when it was time to celebrate these with his grandchildren.

He had been diagnosed with cancer in 1992, just a month before our youngest son's Bar Mitzvah but insisted on coming to Chicago for the ceremony, even though it meant that he would have to discontinue his chemotherapy treatment. I knew how important this coming of age ceremony was to him, and could not dissuade him from attending. I made an appointment for him at the Kellogg Cancer Center hoping I could make some kind of an arrangement to continue his treatment.

After only a few minutes of talking to my Dad, Dr. G. very quietly asked him about the number tattooed on his arm. The doctor's whole family had also perished in the Holocaust, he told us, and he grew up without grandparents, uncles, aunts, or cousins. Before we left, Dr. G. embraced my father and told me not to worry—he would make sure that treatments would start the next day. He was there to greet Dad and explained the procedure every time we came. He told us he considered it a privilege to help a survivor of the Holocaust.

Just before the Bar Mitzvah, Dad asked me if I could talk to his youngest grandson on his behalf. His English was not good enough, he said, but he wanted to explain to him why, after what happened to our family during the Holocaust, it was so important to him that his children and grandchildren never doubt who they are. That they honor the Jewish culture and continue to carry on the traditions even if they do not practice religion. I was a little surprised because Dad never told me exactly what happened to his family. Sensing my surprise, Dad began by apologizing:

"Dziubuś, I should have done more, should have talked to you about how important it is to know who you are, especially in our case. I mean in the case of all Jews, to know what it means to be Jewish not just to others, but to yourself. That it is even more important for a child of two Holocaust survivors. As you know, I've never liked talking about what I went through during the war, but there are some things that your children need to hear. I still don't think that I can handle having this conversation, so I am asking you to do it for me. The Holocaust was something horrible and nothing like this should ever be allowed to happen again.

I feel what's most important and should be stressed over and over, is that the Holocaust was unique. Most people insist on comparing it to other genocides, but what they don't understand, or refuse to see, is that the Nazis' sole aim was to eradicate all Jews, not just from their country but from the world. They were relentless and did not care whether the Jews practiced their religion or not, whether they served in the armies or how much they had contributed to the culture of their respective countries. It did not matter if they looked, talked and behaved like everyone else—the only thing that mattered was that they were JEWS.

How can anyone compare the Holocaust to other genocides? During the six years of WWII, the Nazis slaughtered almost 90 percent of all European Jews. Although we have survived, I am afraid that others will try again, so we must do everything in our power to prevent anything like that from happening again. But we cannot achieve that unless, first, we Jews learn to respect ourselves and are not embarrassed by our identity. And we can never forget what has happened!

I am not religious; I am a Jew because simply because I was born one. And because I value being part of this hard-working and family-oriented society. I truly love our culture, traditions and celebrations, like Bar Mitzvah and Bat Mitzvah. Not for religious reasons, but because these ceremonies and celebrations salute and honor our people and our traditions"

He continued "You are now a mother and I am so relieved to see that you understood how important all this has always been to me, especially after what I went through. But I hope that you will make your children understand that as well. It might sound silly to you, but I feel that abandoning these Jewish traditions would not only make Hitler smile in his grave but would dishonor those who perished and, especially, those of us who were kept alive by our determination to live and carry on our Jewish traditions."

At some point after the Bar Mitzvah ceremony, my father casually mentioned that he, too, had a Bar Mitzvah, but, unfortunately, his brother did not live long enough to have one. This was the first time he had spoken of his brother, so I seized the moment and begged him to please tell me about his family and what happened to them. He hesitated, and for a moment it seemed as if he would, but then he remained silent. Later, just before he left for Australia, he sat down with me and said he was ready to talk about the Holocaust.

He was quick to warn me that his brain had been damaged severely when he was beaten by the Germans, and he couldn't remember most of the names, places, or dates. I had known for a long time that he had this problem, but had no real knowledge of the circumstances leading to this trauma. Hearing that he had been severely beaten, I became a little apprehensive. He had already suffered a heart attack and was under great strain from the cancer treatment. I was worried that what he was about to tell me might be too much for him.

"Daddy," I said, "if this is going to be too hard on you, you don't have to, I understand."

In response, he only smiled and it was obvious he was ready to begin.

The Barber of Auschwitz

He began by telling me about his family and his warm smile slowly faded from his face as he continued:

My family comes from Turek, a small town right next to Kalisz, your Mommy's hometown. My grandparents were observant Jews, but my parents, unlike their ancestors or many of the other Jewish inhabitants of their little town, only attended synagogue on High Holidays. Even though they considered themselves fairly assimilated, they still followed most of the traditions and celebrated every Jewish Holiday at home. Their first language was Polish, which they spoke with each other and with us, but they insisted that their children also learn Yiddish, so they could communicate with their grandparents and the rest of the family.

When it was time to go to school, my brother, my sister, and I were first sent to Cheder, a Jewish school, where in addition to academic subjects, we had religious instruction and learned Yiddish. Although our parents felt it was important for us to be steeped in the language and traditions of our Jewish ancestry, after four years at that school, they thought we were ready for a regular Polish education. It was very important for them to make sure that their children feel equally comfortable in the Polish and Jewish environments.

While most of their friends were Jewish, many were not. My father conducted business as freely with the Gentiles as with Jews and my parents prided themselves on being active members of the Turek community. Their non-Jewish neighbors, the Kowalskis, the Kaminskis, and Jan and Maria, the farmers from whom they bought meat for their butchering business, were among their best friends.

They were especially close with Jan and his wife Maria. In their early forties, they were childless and were terribly fond of me and my sister, but especially of Robert, my brother, who was the youngest. They would often jokingly suggest they would gladly adopt him, especially when my mother complained about his excessive energy. Nothing seemed to give Jan and Maria greater joy than when our family came to visit, and they could watch Robert try to milk the cows, play with the various animals on their farm, and just "breathe the fresh country air." In fact, we all had a good time whenever we got together, and both families considered themselves very lucky, indeed.

All this ended abruptly when Germany invaded Poland and the German troops marched into Turek. The first thing the Germans did was confiscate all Jewish businesses. Soon after, "Judenfrei" signs were painted on every store's window. Jews were forbidden to enter any public facilities and Jewish children could not attend any of the schools. Life became very hard for all the Jews in town, especially when food could no longer be purchased from stores owned by Gentiles. They could still buy it from the farmers who came to town once a week to sell their goods in the open market, but money was scarce, and many of the farmers, antisemites at heart, now refused to sell to "Christ-killers."

Hunger became common and many of the older Jews got sick and some died. The situation was getting worse by the day. Some of the people in town tried to help, but most pretended not to be aware of the situation. Nine months later, all the Jews were ordered to leave their homes, pack one suitcase per family, and report the next day to the town square. They were told that they were all going to be transported to a better place, where they could stay together with other Jews. That same evening, notices warning that hiding or helping the Jews would be punished by death were plastered all over town.

There was a horrendous panic, for rumors of overcrowded ghettos, hard labor camps, and even death camps had been circulating for a couple of months now. Our whole family got together and decided that my brother and I, the two youngest males, should separate from the family and go into hiding right away. But where?

The warning that anyone hiding or helping Jews would be put to death clearly eliminated any possibility of asking Gentile friends for shelter. My parents thought of a spot secluded enough and warm enough where we could stay until all this blew over. They were convinced it would not be long before the boys could return home. An underground potato storage, at the edge of Jan and Maria's farm, where all the boys in our family loved playing hide n' seek in the summer seemed like a good choice, for the farmers accessed it only towards the end of winter, when they began to run out of potatoes in their homes. The family also agreed that they would entrust all their assets, including cash, jewelry and furs to the care of their neighbors and good friends, the Kaminskis.

The two of us, each with a little sack stuffed with food, and some cash sewn into our coats, set off right then, but not before I swore to my parents that we would not leave the shelter for at least three days, and that I would always take care of my little brother. It had just started snowing when we left the house, but, within a very short time, we found ourselves in the middle of a blizzard. At first, enchanted by the whiteness of that very first snow of the season, we thought it would be fun walking alone, in the middle of the night. But we soon realized how dangerous that journey might be. The Germans were everywhere, patrolling the area on motorcycles and on foot. We had to move very quietly, avoiding major streets. Two hours later, with the field still nowhere in sight, Robert, by then very tired, became cranky and refused to walk any further and, ditching my food sack, I carried him the rest of the way to the potato storage.

For three days we did not leave the shelter, even though the food that Robert had in his sack barely lasted for two. Though potatoes were plentiful, we had no matches to light a fire and even if we had, we did not want to chance attracting attention. On the fourth day, under the cover of darkness, I decided to take a chance and set off to procure some food. I had no idea how to go about it. I had money but going to town was out of the question. I contemplated approaching Jan, whose farm was right there, but decided against it, heeding our parents' admonitions not to endanger any friends.

After a while, I figured that it would be OK to "borrow" some eggs and maybe even get some milk from Jan's barn. I knew the family would not mind if they knew that my brother and I needed the food. But the barn was locked and I had to go back empty-handed. I hoped that the next day might be luckier. But, whenever I attempted to leave the hiding place, I heard noises outside that sounded like motorcycles, and terrified that the Germans might be on the lookout for runaway Jews, I stayed put. Robert and I did not have any food but we were at least able to quench our thirst by licking snow. When my brother complained about hunger, I made him pretend we were sitting at a holiday table and quizzed him about the delicacies our mother prepared for the Jewish New Year.

Unfortunately, it did not work and he would fall asleep crying. I realized that I had to take a risk and find some food no matter what.

As I was about to leave, the flap of the shelter opened and I came eye to eye with Jan, who, pushing me down, motioned to be quiet. Jan left quickly after taking out some of the potatoes and whispered that he would come back later. That night he appeared with plenty of food, a couple of blankets, and a whole big canister full of milk. He explained that he heard all the Jews were deported, but was also told that my brother and I were not with the rest of the family. He figured we went into hiding and he started looking for us. He remembered that we, and Robert especially, always liked to play hide and seek in the potato storage. But a German garrison had been stationed in his house and the soldiers stayed up very late and he didn't want to draw their suspicions by leaving the house at night. But then Maria suggested serving them lots of vodka, they fell into a drunken stupor, and so he felt it was safe to check. He explained that as long as the Germans were staying in his house, he could not take us in, but he would deliver food and more milk whenever he could. For a month he came regularly, always with food and milk.

One day he told us that he was off to a neighboring town to attend the funeral of his wife's sister and on the way back would stop to take Robert home with them. He and Maria decided they would tell everybody that Robert was the deceased sister's son and that since she was widowed, and there was no one else to look after him, Jan and Maria would now raise him as their own. They were sure no one would suspect anything, and that they could get away with it, especially since Robert now looked like a completely different person. He had lost a lot of weight and no longer resembled the chubby child the village might have remembered. Shaving off his curly hair would complete the transformation and would not draw attention since most of the young children in the surrounding area had their hair cropped because of a lice epidemic.

Fate was kind to us all. On Jan's return, the Germans were gone, having moved to better accommodation in town. Robert moved in without a hitch. I stayed in the shelter only during the day, afraid of being seen by the help, but at night, convinced by Jan and Maria that this was better for Robert, I would come to the house to wash and sleep. Whenever I expressed fear that they could be executed if the Germans found me in their home and tried to leave, or, even when they sensed my apprehension about staying on, Jan and Maria assured me that they took every precaution and they knew what they were doing. They told me over and over not to think about them, that they were doing what was right and would not have it any other way. No matter the consequences, they were willing to take the chance. They insisted that anyone valuing human life would do the same and their only regret was that they did not find out about the deportation in time to hide the whole family.

Everything worked according to plan until one sunny spring day, when the Germans' dogs found me. I was dragged out from the shelter, kicked and severely beaten. I was then taken to the train station, and thrown together with the other Jewish prisoners who apparently hid in the neighboring forest. The Germans suspected that Jan and Maria, as well as the other farmers who lived near the forests, knew about those Jews and were ordered to bring all their horses and come with their families to the train station the next morning. All the animals were shot right there.

For some reason, they also thought that I knew about other Jews still hiding in the area. When I denied it, I was beaten, right there in front of the local families, including Jan, Maria, and my little brother, still pretending to be their son. They punched and kicked me and my head was smashed on the cobblestones. Seeing that, my brother pulled away from Maria, shouted "Stop hitting my brother" and ran towards me. He was shot instantly. I lost consciousness and when I came to, I was in a cattle car heading for Auschwitz. I never learned what happened to Jan and Maria.

I was unable to move and was in a lot of pain. My head was in the lap of a man I had never met before and when I looked up, he told me his name was Alek. I was weak and in pain and Alek kept helping me all through the journey. But after a while, even he got weak—there was no food but worse, there was no water. At one point, the train suddenly slowed down and I saw some farmers in the fields. I crawled to the bars and stretched my hands out through the slats. I waved frantically, and, as loud as I could, begged for some water. Not one of the farmers moved towards the train. Standing still, as if they had rehearsed it, each and every one raised one hand and drew their fingers across their throats. It was an awful sight but even worse was the realization that a cattle car filled with people being transported for slaughter, did not elicit pity or even sympathy. Instead, they all roared with laughter.

By the time we arrived at our destination, I was able to walk on my own. Alek and I were assigned to the same quarters and shared the same bunk bed with three other men. During the day we all went off to different assignments, but every evening we talked and tried to keep each other's spirits up. Hungry all the time, cold, exhausted and terribly scared, we watched helplessly as, day after day, men who were too weak to work were shot right in front of our eyes. The realization that any day that same fate might befall me was omnipresent. But, I never lost hope.

At times when life might have become unbearable, I thought back to all the happy occasions I celebrated with family and friends. I remembered all the good deeds my family had done for others and told myself over and over that there are many others like them, as confirmed by Jan and Maria. I knew that in order to survive, I had to still believe that good will always defeat evil. However, the evidence to the contrary was everywhere I looked. I resisted giving in to despair. Instead, every morning and every night before I went to sleep, I kept repeating that I am strong, that I can cope with any situation, that in order to survive, I have to stop constantly looking around me.

One evening, after I had been in Auschwitz for some time, the chief guard, whose name I can't recall, dragged me outside, and barked "You are the new barber and if you don't do your job well or screw up even once, I will kill you, is that clear?"

I wondered what happened to the other barber but knew better than to ask. I also knew the last barber got more food, so without lifting my head and in the meekest manner I could think of, I said "I presume that there will be many new prisoners coming in every day, and perhaps it would be faster and much more efficient to have another person help me? I know my bunkmate Alek would be really right for this job—he is a hard worker and very obedient."

He was furious and took great pleasure in pushing me down and kicking me. But even though these were very painful, I just clenched my teeth and waited. I did not lift my head. Eventually, he barked "Go back right now before I kill you."

The next morning, he came and, without looking at me, said "Get the other filthy Jew" but quickly added "He is your responsibility—he does not do his job, you are both dead."

When I brought Alek, he handed us each a sack filled with razors, belts and soap. But there were no scissors. How was I supposed to cut hair with just a razor? Alek and I looked at each other and, when the guard walked away, I asked "How are we supposed to cut hair without scissors?"

"I think we are meant to shave it all off."

Alek and I worked all day long. Neither we nor the prisoners we shaved got any water or food and at the end of the day, I was so thirsty, I felt that I couldn't even swallow. My stomach, too, was letting me know that I was not well, but I knew I had no choice. Alek was not well either, but we both thought better than to complain. To my surprise, just a few days later, I got two extra slices of bread and something the guard called soup. I drank the soup right away in front of the guard but as soon as he left, I shared the bread with Alek.

We both worked all day long and soon became robot-like—that way we were able to perform our duties without thought or feelings. During the day I was somehow able to ignore the abominations that surrounded me. At night, when the nightmares woke me, I just kept repeating to myself "I am strong, I will survive no matter what."

When the two slices of bread were reduced to one and I could no longer control the constant hunger that corroded my stomach, I forced myself to remember my house and the happy times with family. But hunger was never my worst enemy. Far more dangerous, despite all the various tactics I learned to employ, was the feeling of enormous hopelessness and despair when I thought of what evil deeds human beings were capable of; how, no matter how principled or noble people thought themselves to be, given certain conditions, even the loftiest of their ideals were so easily compromised.

I could not stop myself from wondering if there was any good reason for wanting to stay alive. To live among people who did not protest when their friends and neighbors were deprived of basic human rights; who stood silent while they saw fellow humans whose only crime was being Jewish, being herded like animals into cattle cars to concentration camps where they were gassed en masse? To remember babies who were thrown to the dogs that were intentionally kept starving just for that purpose, or to see in my dreams those tiny humans smashed against brick walls like they were nothing but garbage? To keep wondering how these guards, often parents themselves, have been capable of ripping children away from their mothers and then shooting them right there?

Please believe me when I tell you, at such times I felt that I could never again believe in the existence of basic good. But what kept me sane at times like these was the memory of Jan and Maria. Their bravery, kindness and endless generosity; their willingness to do anything, to sacrifice their lives to protect and save a fellow human. Jan and Maria were my magical tool, a beautiful portrait from the past that kept me from drowning in the abyss which could have engulfed me. But how many Jan and Marias were out there? The Holocaust is a perfect example of how easily human beings can be manipulated and even infected by evil. Hitler's followers were not all stupid or uneducated, and yet most of them willingly supported his obsession to eradicate all Jews from this earth. I say most, because undoubtedly there were people who opposed his actions but, even among those, there were only a few who had the courage to openly stand up to the Nazis.

I often ask myself—what sets people like Jan and Maria apart? Why would they risk their lives and defy such orders? Was it high moral principles, deep religious beliefs, or just sheer respect for human lives? And, are traits innate or can they be learned? How is it that, swept by Hitler's enthusiastic rhetoric, university professors, teachers, lawyers and even doctors abandoned their principles? Even committed heinous crimes and behaved like monsters. How is something like this possible?

Dziubuś, please ask yourself—isn't it very important to ask such questions now, especially for those who teach about the Holocaust? And isn't it just as important to consider the role antisemitism played in all those horrific events? To make your children realize that if we continue to ignore it, something like this can happen again?

Turning Points

What causes this worldwide disdain for the Jews? I distinctly remember a discussion I had with a young graduate student at the University of Illinois. When he found out that I was Jewish, he, like many before him, expressed surprise. When I asked him why, he meekly told me that I look like any other Polish woman and not like a Jew. So I asked "What does a Jew look like?"

"Well, I always heard that they have crooked noses and dark, curly hair"

"And that is why people don't like them?" I asked.

"Well, no. Mostly they don't like that most of them speak with a Jewish accent," then, head hanging down, truly embarrassed, he added quietly "Actually, nobody likes Jews because they are money grabbers and are dishonest."

"Anything else?" I asked.

Almost in a whisper, he told me "Well, I also heard that they all smell of garlic," but quickly added "Maybe this is only true of the Polish Jews?"

As gently as I could, I explained to him that such an attitude, among other misconceptions, is characteristic of antisemites. We talked for a long time about some of the other stereotypes attached to Jews. At some point, this young man, with tears in his eyes, said "Oh my God, I am an antisemite! And so is my whole family! I am too embarrassed to tell you what else I have heard all my life about Jews and how my family feels about them! Thank you for pointing all this out to me. I wish there was a course on antisemitism in every school!"

"I do too," I told him.

Today, looking at the resurgence of antisemitic sentiment in Europe, it feels like this might be a good place to start. My father's warning stands stark in my mind, and is somehow more relevant than ever before. If we don't learn anything from our past mistakes, how long will it be before something like the Holocaust happens again? What can we really do to stop it?

At a young age, I had no idea what a Jew was, let alone that I was one. When my best friend's mother screamed that no filthy Jew would touch their blessed Easter basket, I looked around for the filthy person, not for a minute suspecting she was referring to me.

Once, at a sleepover at my friend's grandma's house. While we were getting ready for bed and I was trying to brush out my very unruly, chestnut hair, the grandma walked in. "What unusually curly hair you have," she said, "If I didn't know better, I would have thought you were a *Zydoweczka* (Jewess), but who knows, maybe you are?"

She looked at me suspiciously and something about it frightened me. The next morning at breakfast and throughout that day she gave the same strange look and constantly mumbled something under her breath. I cannot remember if I said anything to her at all, but when I related this incident to my mother, she dismissed it with a wave and a shrug and told me to forget it. And yet, every evening after that, she relentlessly brushed my hair, trying to straighten it and pulling on it so hard that I had tears in my eyes. I heard her mumble, "Thank goodness it's only your hair."

Why didn't my mom explain to me what this was all about? Then or later?

I now realize that the anger I began to feel toward my mother was rooted in her attitude toward our Jewish identity. She could invent such wonderful tales about any subject but would not give me even the barest description of any part of our culture. Where were her vivid imaginative interpretations of the stories that are important to me as a Jew? In her lack of engagement with our culture, she had denied me the opportunity to develop my own identity and my feelings about my Jewishness. It took a very long time and many turning points for me to come to any sort of understanding that made me at ease with my Jewish identity. And, maybe this is another reason that the secret is so fixed in my mind. What else might she have kept from me and why?

For the fifteen years that I lived in Poland, I never thought of myself as different and so did not at any time feel conflicted about my identity. I knew that I was Jewish, but at that time it meant nothing to me. Throughout my childhood, Mom made a point of telling me how "No one in our family, not I, you or Daddy in any way resemble those Jews who speak Yiddish and don't speak Polish well." I presume that she thought I was too young to understand that some people are closed-minded, that they hate for no reason, or maybe she thought that she was protecting me. But shouldn't she have told me about antisemitism at some point?

Did she really want me to believe that I will be liked and will stay safe because I don't look Jewish? Had she forgotten that her classic Aryan looks did not stop the Nazis from coming for her, and did not stop them from sending her to Łódź ghetto and then to Auschwitz? That not one of them was fooled by her blonde hair, blue eyes, patrician nose, and high cheekbones? That it did not matter to them that she spoke "upper class," "educated Polish," or, worse still, that, like them, she could not tolerate anyone who had even the slightest Yiddish accent and that she spoke of those Jews with as much disdain as if they were vermin? How could she not understand that to the Nazis, regardless of her own strong feelings of Polishness, she was just another filthy Jew? Is it possible that my mother did not realize that this would be a good lesson to teach a Jewish child? Was she truly so ashamed of being Jewish? Or did she never think about it?

My mother's pride in her Aryan looks and her perfect language skills made it very hard for anyone, especially a Polish person, to believe that she was Jewish. Inevitably, they would ask "I know your husband is Jewish but you aren't, right? You look like any of us and you use our language far better than most Polish people. And you just don't behave like most of the Jews I know. I am right, no"?

Mom would smile and say, "Think about it, Poland is where I was born and raised, and so were my parents and grandparents and no one in my family spoke Yiddish. I am as much of a Pole as you are."

I heard this response many times, but one particular time, while I was visiting my parents in Australia when I heard her say this to a Polish carpenter who was doing some work on my parents' kitchen, it angered me. I thought of the many occasions when instead of just confirming that she was Jewish, she felt the need to somehow justify herself. Why? She now lived in a country where so many of its citizens came from other countries, spoke other languages, and practiced different religions? In fact, many Australian citizens did not resemble their Caucasian brethren, and yet none were embarrassed by it. More importantly, she lived in a country where, unlike in Poland, no matter whether you were a Jew or a Muslim, or if you practiced religion or none, once you became a citizen, you were automatically regarded as an Australian and this was clearly stated in all legal documents.

In Poland, Mom would often say that she had an undying love for her Polishness and when asked to explain, she would then quote her favorite Jewish/Polish poet, Julian Tuwim "My homeland is the Polish language." But couldn't an intelligent person like my mother shake off the need to assure people that she was not like the other Jews? Was she like all those antisemites who regarded Jews as somehow inferior? The more I thought about it, the angrier I became at her until a disturbing thought struck me "Am I any different?"

I, too, just like my mother, had felt disdain for those who spoke Polish or English with a Yiddish accent and, just like her, I had often tried to prove that I had nothing in common with "those Jews." This revelation was an awakening and the beginning of a new me. It had been so much easier to blame my mother and stay angry with her, instead of facing the fact that I was always her sycophant and had not given myself permission to think for myself. That conversation between my mother and the Polish handyman was the first turning point on the road to taking responsibility for my choices and becoming my own person. But it also revealed something deeper—it made me see my own fragility, my dependence on Mother's approval and acceptance.

Until I moved to the USA I was not aware that most Jews, those who still live in Poland and those who migrated to other countries, believe that hatred, or a deep contempt for the Jews, has always been the zeitgeist of Polish culture. They feel such attitudes did not diminish, even after WWII, when very few Jews were left. More so, they believe that those attitudes remain strong today. I also did not know that it was, and probably still is, common for many Poles, as is often the case with certain corners of Christianity, to blame Jews for Christ's death; that they say that matzo is made with Christian children's blood; that all Jews are greedy, dirty and forever smelling of garlic; that they all have crooked noses, dark curly hair, beady brown eyes, and are not trustworthy; and, more importantly, that if you are born a Jew, you can never be Polish.

While it is certainly an exaggeration that all Polish people feel that way about Jews, it is a fact that, at least when I lived there, no one who was not a Catholic, or at least not a Christian, was considered to be a Pole—not just by his fellow citizens but by the authorities, as it was ethnicity that defined one's nationality. Official applications, whether for primary school or university, for a passport or in order to join any organization, etc., had a question about nationality, and under that question, "Jew" was listed separately to "Polish." Thus, all citizens who were Jewish, even those whose Polish ancestry went back hundreds of years, were still expected to answer such a question with "JEW." I was barely fifteen when I left and had never given a thought to any of that. But much later, when I had already moved to the USA, I asked my mother "Why did you stay in Poland for such a long time?"

"I was born there and it was the only country I knew. I spent my childhood there, I was educated there, knew its history, spoke the language, and loved it. I got married and gave birth to you there. It was my world and I did not belong anywhere else!"

I understood that part and so I asked her "But why do you always have such aversion to simply stating, 'I may not look Jewish but I am?' Most of my friends, especially those who left Poland in the1960s, still take great pride in using the Polish language correctly, have fond memories of their native country and from their past and yet none would allow a Polish person to think that not looking Jewish was a compliment."

My mother sat silent and did not respond.

"Mommy," I continued, "You know that many of my friends came to America in 1968. Because they are Jewish, they were stripped of their citizenship and forced to leave Poland? They were educated there; some even have PhDs. They loved the country as much as you did and to this day think of Poland as their birth country. Like you, they love the Polish language and speak it better than they do English; they speak with nostalgia about the forests where they hunted for mushrooms and, like you, pine for the dunes and the Baltic sea they swam in. They also reminisce fondly about the Tatra Mountains where they skied in the winter or where they attended summer camp. And yet every one of them would respond 'I know you don't realize it, but it is pretty offensive when you ask: Are you really Jewish because you don't look like one!'

"You will never understand, will you?" she responded angrily and left the room.

I remember sharing that conversation with my best friend and her husband, both of whom were forced to leave Poland in 1968. They told me about the many antisemitic remarks they ignored when they were children, because antisemitism was not something they were aware of or, because these were made by people who were highly educated and considered to be "intellectuals." Using a diminutive like "Czy może Pani jest Zydoweczka?" (Miss, are you by any chance a Jewess?) they made sure that you knew you were suspect if you were a Jew, but also that you would not be offended if you were not. Others, like colleagues at work, or university professors, would take an even more subtle approach, "Czy moze Pani/Pan jest Mojzeszowego wyznania?" (Miss/Sir, is there a chance that you might be of the Moses faith?)

Speaking of these sly comments, my girlfriend added "The question itself might not seem offensive to a non-Jew. But we, Jews, immediately recognized the suspicious tone and the venom with which such seemingly insignificant words were spat out. It always made me shudder."

At that point, all I could think of was the tone of Mom's voice whenever she retold the story of her first shopping trip to a local fruit store, not long after we arrived in Australia. She wanted to buy some grapes and began picking out the nicest ones from the display. The owner stopped her and pointed to the ones on the shelf inside the store. But Mom did not like the way they looked, told him that in Polish, since she knew no English, and proceeded to bag the grapes she already had in her hand. The Jewish owner, according to my mother, chased her out screaming in Yiddish, "Polish Madama, du vilst vinogrohnen? gei somewhere else."

She would always wince with great distaste as she repeated the word "vinogrohnen," rolling the rrrs and prolonging the ohs to make her point. At no time did she make fun of, or express any contempt for the man's lack of respect for his customers. The thing that most offended her was his Yiddish. I heard this story a few times over the years, but it was not until one particular day, after I had been reflecting on my identity and antisemitism for a long time, that I suddenly understood why my father never stayed to join in the laughter that followed, but, instead, walked out of the room as soon as Mom began to tell the story. If I did not have so much proof to the contrary, I might even believe that she was not a Jew herself and that was *the* secret.

Is it possible that even after all she had been through, she still believed that by behaving this way she would, in the future, prevent anything bad happening to her again? Or to me? Or was this delusion keeping her sane? Like the world she created and lived in? One that specifically suited her own sensibilities? Is that why we always had a choinka, known as a Christmas tree in English-speaking countries, and yet she never taught me anything about Hanukkah, Passover, or Rosh Hashanah?

I distinctly recall our family's first Passover dinner, in Australia and how stunned I was when our hostess served dishes that Mom had prepared every year to celebrate what she called a "special Spring celebration." First came a mixture of apples, walnuts, wine and honey, which the hostess called haroset, then a stuffed carp, which she called gefilte fish, which was accompanied by a dish of carrots, cooked with apples and prunes, called tzimmes. When Mrs. B. brought in my favorite, a feathery light sponge cake, and asked me if I would like some lekach, I asked if that was an English word for that kind of cake and asked her to please repeat all the English names of the previous dishes, so I could learn their proper names in my new country.

"No, dear," she said sweetly, "these are not English but Yiddish names for those traditional Passover dishes."

"Traditional Passover food?" I looked at my mom.

She gave me a strange look, smiled and said, "But Anitus, (*that is what Mom called me*) that is exactly what I made these for"

"But Mommy, we didn't celebrate any Jewish Holidays in Poland!"

She shook her head and said in a voice filled with pity "Anitus, you couldn't have been this naive—we did celebrate every Jewish Holiday! Why would I have made lekach without any flour, if not for Passover? Or, haroset? And the honey cake and apples dipped in honey—why, if not for Rosh Hashanah?"

I was speechless and did not know how to respond. We did, indeed, have all the delicacies she mentioned, but at no time did I hear any mention of Passover or Rosh Hashanah. But there was no use pursuing that conversation. Unlike other occasions when Mom behaved as if I had missed something and made me feel angry, this time I was happy. I thought that from now on, not only I, but Mom would also feel comfortable with "those Jews." She liked our Australian hosts a lot, even though they looked exactly like the ones Mom always talked about with such disdain. I was thrilled! I guess that is why I thought that evening was the point I finally became comfortable with my Jewish identity, but, when I think about it now, it took far longer.

After I got married and we moved to New York, I met many other children of Holocaust survivors. And once again, just like when I first arrived in Australia, I felt a strange yet similar bond with them. At that time, I began to feel a pressing need to learn more about the Holocaust and that urge soon bordered on obsession. By the time I had all of my three children, I had read Primo Levi, many testimonials written by Holocaust survivors, and watched many movies that dealt with the subject. The more I read, the more I realized that the Holocaust was a culminating point of a long history of disdain, of contempt, and pure hatred; a time when even the most rational people, those educated in the tradition of Schiller and Goethe, doctors who took the Hippocratic oath, were willing to murder people whose only crime had been a different religion or sometimes just traditions, since not Jews all were religious.

That is when I understood why it had been so important to my father that his children and grandchildren feel unabashed about their Jewish identity and why he tried so hard to make me understand that. Because of him, even though I still thought of myself as a Polish Jew and not a Jew born in Poland, I knew I was never going to marry a man who was not Jewish. When our first son was born, I insisted that he was going to be circumcised. When they got older I was adamant that each of our children attend Sunday school and that our boys would become a Bar Mitzvah and daughter a Bat Mitzvah. I did all that even though the actual rituals meant nothing to me, and, if asked, I could not have explained why I loved them. I think now that I felt it was my responsibility not just to my father, but to my children as well. But now I know that the main reason for my insistence might have been because I felt a strong need to give our children something I never had—a chance to understand the traditions, and, when they were old enough, to have the choice and decide for themselves who they are and who they want to be.

My determination became ever stronger after we moved from NY to Chicago. We rented a house in a lovely development. Our next-door neighbor welcomed us with cookies and gave me the name of the neighborhood babysitter; who came the next day to babysit while I went grocery shopping. Even though I knew no other people in Chicago, I did not feel lonely and felt I could easily make friends with my neighbors and the parents of my children's classmates. My girlfriends from NY called every day to make sure I was OK. To make me feel at home, one of them sent a beautiful Mezuzah for our new dwelling. Like me, she was not a religious person, so we did not kiss it as we entered our homes, but she and I shared the feeling that it was important to have it on our front door. I was nailing it onto the door of our Chicago residence, when my friendly neighbor, Susan, came over to chat. She wanted to know what it was and I explained. She was surprised to hear that I was Jewish and stayed for just a few more minutes before going back.

Two days later, my husband and I decided it would be nice to go out for dinner next Saturday, so I called the babysitter Susan recommended, to see if she could come. There was a short silence before she told me that she was not available.

"Could you come on Sunday, instead?" I asked.

"No, I'm afraid I cannot," she replied.

I did not think anything of it and asked what was the best day for her to babysit.

"I am afraid I will not be able to babysit for you at all—I am not allowed to work for Jews" and she hung up. I was deeply disturbed but another incident made me even more so.

A year or so later, I got a job as a court interpreter. On my first day, I received a very warm reception from all my colleagues and was invited to share the pizza they bought for lunch. We shared some basic information like the cities in Poland we each came from, our marital status, children, etc. Then, someone asked where I was living at the time. When I answered Northbrook, one of the women gasped and uttered with horror "Oh, you poor thing! With all those Jews?"

Before I could say anything, another Polish interpreter, Margot, took my hand, led me out of the room, and said "I am so sorry, they are such a bunch of bloody antisemites, just ignore them."

I did, but it was hard. However, Margot and I became very good friends, worked well together, and spent a lot of time together after work as well. One day, she asked me "I am curious—You do not go to synagogue, you still speak Polish at home with your husband and, even though you speak pretty good English, you say that Polish is your first language and that you still count in Polish. Your closest friends come from Poland, so what is it that makes you Jewish?"

I was taken off guard. I didn't know what to say, because I never had the need to verbalize it. "To tell you the truth," I replied, "I don't know how to answer that question except that I just am and know it."

Margot smiled, hugged me, and never touched that subject again.

Why didn't I think about it more? This wasn't the first time I had heard that question, and yet I could not come up with a satisfactory answer for a very long time. I read somewhere that when one struggles to make sense of one's life, sometimes just one moment, a single event seemingly ordinary, can offer a sudden understanding of something that otherwise could be lost. I wonder which, if any of these turning points, was the moment I understood? Maybe we are never really meant to fully make sense of our own lives, but rather continuously renegotiate our meanings, narrowing in on those that are truly most important to us.

For much of my life, I was very much my magical mommy's sycophant, though of course, I did not realize it. If it took many years for me to simply step out of the shadow of my mother, is it any wonder that she struggled to step out of the shadow of her own past and the anguish it might have caused her? As I am now still struggling to unravel my mother's secret, I wonder if I'm still languishing in the shade of my mother's world without even realizing it? Still unable to find that castle in the sky that has been so elusive?

Though I still have not succeeded thus in uncovering the secret, a more important truth has become ever more clear: my conflict with my mother and, possibly, my preoccupation with the secret, is tied to finding who I am, to my identity. If writing this book, and examining my own past, has led to anything, it is an understanding of why it is so important to me that my children and grandchildren never feel ambiguous about their identity. As my father said, we must understand who we are and stand up for ourselves if we are to preserve our fragile place in this world. I feel that this is ever more important with every passing day.

Revelations

At a pivotal point during writing this book, during my quest to unravel the secret, I suddenly faced a crisis of confidence. Not only had my mother kept some kind of secret from me but the little she did tell me about her childhood might not have been true. It was also possible that my own background wasn't even what I thought it was. The probability of discovering the secret had become incredibly slim. How could I continue writing when every certainty was suddenly in doubt? In the midst of that panic, I reminded myself of the advice my cousin's wife, Monique, gave me at the family reunion in Poland.

"Press the delete button on the unknown, tell them what you were told and write your story—a story of a child of two Holocaust survivors"

And, that is what I did. Since I could not write a memoir, this book became my story; not a fiction but a pastiche, a kaleidoscopic pattern of events shared by my mother and father, but related by me, how I remember them. However, since I have now become increasingly cognizant of how fickle and easily malleable all memories really are, I cannot truly guarantee the veracity of my own memories, let alone those of others. Some of my parents' stories were incomplete, missing important details. Even though it felt like something was missing in my life, and this void often made me sad and still does, I did not probe. I recognized the pain such questions caused and followed my instincts not to pry. I still think my feelings were right. Recording even the little they shared and carefully examining it, helped me understand the reasons for the omissions. It also made me comprehend why my mother had such an overwhelming need to keep inventing alternate "realities."

I realized that even though my parents always thought of themselves as survivors and never as victims, they were deeply affected by what happened to them, and so was I, even though I did not know it. Now, I am convinced more than ever, that all Jews, myself included, must stand unabashedly in front of those who would hate and deride us. I hope that by reading everything that I have recorded, my own family will be able to see that the Holocaust and Never Again are no longer as powerful they once were; as horrific and urgent as these used to sound, they have sadly become nothing more than banal terms. More importantly, I hope that they see that antisemitism still not only exists but is on the rise and as dangerous as ever. I have shared my parents' stories in their own voices, because, from my own experience, I found that first-hand experiences and personal accounts affect and resonate better than any history lesson or history book. They provide a more direct link, especially when these horrific things happened to members of your own family.

Camus, in his novel, The Plague, describes an epidemic that decimates a small town. Though not a physical affliction, his words resonate with antisemitism and how it might lead to another Holocaust.

"... he knew what those jubilant crowds did not know but could have learned from books: that the plague bacillus never dies or disappears for good; that it can lie dormant for years ... that it bides its time in bedrooms, cellars, trunks, and bookshelves; and that perhaps the day would come when, for the bane and the enlightening of men, it would rouse up its rats again and send them forth to die in a happy city."

I now feel an urgency to, particularly, help my grandchildren understand this, because I didn't for such a long time. That realization played a pivotal role in my transformation from a naive Polish-Jewish child to an independent thinking adult; from a Polish Jew, always conflicted and ambiguous about her identity, to a Jew born and raised in Poland. Regrettably, my reconnection with my Jewish identity partly led to my disillusionment with my magical mommy and caused a rift between us. I am now filled with guilt and remorse. I should have understood the reasons for her ambiguity about her identity or why she could not accept this new version of myself, no longer her little acolyte. I should have been more tolerant and should have made sure that despite all our problems, she knew that I never stopped loving her.

Such revelations, including those concerning the importance of recognizing and countering antisemitism and those regarding my own identity, are all important, but are certainly not the revelations that I thought would be concluding this book. Of course, when I first began, it was my hope that I would be able to reveal the mystery of the secret. Yet I still do not know. I have not been able to find out if my mother actually had a twin, or what really happened to her sister, Dorota, or how or where my grandfather died, or the reason for my grandparents' ten-year separation, or why my mother "borrowed" large parts of her cousins' backgrounds. These questions remain unanswered but certainly not for lack of trying or want.

I recorded all the memories I could, even those that had long been buried before I started writing. I have carefully written down everything, examined all my own memories, and deliberated on everything I have found. I have even speculated and invented scenarios, most of which, thankfully, have proven incorrect, but I still have not been able to fathom a scenario that might solve what the secret holds. And so, the key that would reveal the secret is still missing. But I am reconciled with the thought that even though solving the mystery gave me the original impetus, it was never as important as allowing my children and grandchildren a more personal glimpse of the past, especially about what happened to their great grandparents and family during the Holocaust, and to help them realize that if our society is not vigilant, it can happen again.

So, I am done with the secret, for now at least. But, does that mean that the mystery of the secret should remain unsolved? Will it forever remain distant and unattainable, like some castle in the sky? I cannot decipher the future any more than I've been able to decipher the secret. But, maybe, I can now pass the torch on, so to speak, to my younger family members? Could my older grandchildren, Wolf, Mia, Ephram, and Noa, or maybe at some point in the future, their younger cousins, Kira, Aiden, Emma, Sammie, or Levi, be inspired and solve this secret? Maybe if they see it as a jigsaw puzzle just too hard for their grandmother to complete? Wouldn't that be a fitting tribute to my mother's memory, if her secret became their castle in the sky? And, if it does and they manage to solve it, then my own wish would come true as well.

Would that not be proof that my mother had always been right? That if you hope for something and wish hard enough, that if you believe that your most fervent wish can come true, then it will?

How could we all not be grateful to my mommy?

CPSIA information can be obtained
at www.ICGtesting.com
Printed in the USA
LVHW090347230721
693405LV00003BA/238